The Power of Pleasure

Also by Douglas Weiss, Ph.D.

Intimacy: A 100-Day Guide to Lasting Relationships

*The 7 Love Agreements: Decisions you can make
on your own to strengthen your marriage*

❧

Hay House Titles of Related Interest

*Four Acts of Personal Power: How to Heal Your Past
and Create a Positive Future,* by Denise Linn

*The Heart of Love: How to Go Beyond Fantasy to Find True
Relationship Fulfillment,* by Dr. John F. Demartini

*The Power of Infinite Love & Gratitude: An Evolutionary
Journey to Awakening Your Spirit,* by Dr. Darren R. Weissman

The Power of Touch, by Phyllis K. Davis, Ph.D.

Repotting: 10 Steps for Redesigning Your Life,
by Diana Holman and Ginger Pape

*You Can Have What You Want: Proven Strategies
for Inner and Outer Success,* by Michael Neill

*Your Destiny Switch: Master Your Key Emotions, and
Attract the Life of Your Dreams!* by Peggy McColl

What Color Is Your Personality? by Carol Ritberger, Ph.D.

❧

The Hay House titles above are available at your
local bookstore, or may be ordered by visiting:

Hay House USA: **www.hayhouse.com**®
Hay House Australia: **www.hayhouse.com.au**
Hay House UK: **www.hayhouse.co.uk**
Hay House South Africa: **orders@psdprom.co.za**
Hay House India: **www.hayhouseindia.co.in**

The Power of Pleasure

Maximizing Your Enjoyment for a Lifetime

Douglas Weiss, Ph.D.

HAY HOUSE, INC.
Carlsbad, California
London • Sydney • Johannesburg
Vancouver • Hong Kong • New Delhi

Published and distributed in the United States by: Hay House, Inc.: www.hayhouse.com • *Published and distributed in Australia by:* Hay House Australia Pty. Ltd.: www.hayhouse.com.au • *Published and distributed in the United Kingdom by:* Hay House UK, Ltd.: www.hayhouse.co.uk • *Published and distributed in the Republic of South Africa by:* Hay House SA (Pty), Ltd.: orders@psdprom.co.za • *Distributed in Canada by:* Raincoast: www.raincoast.com • *Published in India by:* Hay House Publishers India: www.hayhouseindia.co.in

Design: Tricia Breidenthal

Library of Congress Cataloging-in-Publication Data

Weiss, Douglas.
    The power of pleasure : maximizing your enjoyment for a lifetime / Douglas Weiss. -- 1st ed.
        p. cm.
    ISBN-13: 978-1-4019-1197-3 (tradepaper) 1. Pleasure. I. Title.
    BF515.W38 2007
    152.4'2--dc22
                                                2006031301

ISBN: 978-1-4019-1197-3

10 09 08 07   4 3 2 1
1st edition, May 2007

Printed in the United States of America

This book is dedicated to
Virginia Schaffer (1923–2006),
who was a pleasure
to every soul she touched.

Contents

Please Note: All of the stories and
case studies in this book are true;
however, all names have been changed
for confidentiality purposes.

Introduction

We all live in a world full of incredible pleasure, yet many of us don't feel as if we're getting enough of it from our life. So often we're working, raising families, having relationships, and taking care of other responsibilities that tend to give us less time for ourselves and our unique pleasures.

You see, as a counselor for more than 18 years, I've regularly seen people who are drained of pleasure. They might call it burnout or sadness or say that they're just not enjoying themselves. *I* call it not having the power of pleasure in their life.

You're about to enter a world of pleasure. This isn't just anyone's pleasure; it's uniquely *yours*. In the following pages, you'll discover exactly what gives you real joy in your life.

We all have limited time for pleasure, so it's important that we experience it fully on a regular basis. Doing so is what makes life fun and enjoyable for all of us. You're holding a guide that can identify, maximize, and actually put into practice your optimal pleasure. Before you finish this book, your life and schedule can become extremely different. Once you recognize what your pleasures are, you'll actually get out your calendar and schedule them in. And as a counselor, I know that if you can get something down on a calendar, it's at least ten times more likely to happen.

You deserve pleasure—actually, you deserve the power of pleasure to be an integral, invisible force in your successful life. There are several secrets to a rewarding life, and the power of pleasure is one of them. Like many such secrets, it's not something that you're taught in school. I'm a perfect example of this: I have four degrees, and I was never offered a class on pleasure!

Strap yourself in for a ride down the river of pleasure. I'll be *your* guide, just as I've helped many others navigate their way along the pleasure river. At the end, you'll find greater energy, more smiles, and a more elevated spirit about the life you'll be *enjoying*—not just living.

So grab *your* oar, and be prepared to paddle through the canyons to discover your pleasure hierarchy. Once you've been down the river, you become your own guide for the rest of your life. Later you'll help others find *their* pleasures, and ultimately you'll become a part of the team of those who have the power of pleasure flowing through their new and happier life.

❁ ❁ ❁

Chapter One

Body Pleasures

From the top of your head to the soles of your feet, you're a pleasure machine. If you don't believe me, have someone massage your scalp or wash your hair—or better yet, get a nice foot rub—and see how much you enjoy it. Yes, you're absolutely, unabashedly, a pleasure machine!

Knowing that you're created for pleasure is critical to living your life to the fullest on planet Earth. Your understanding of your very own pleasure zones and pleasure hierarchy can make everything so much more enjoyable. Not only will your life be better, you'll also live more harmoniously with all those other pleasure machines on the planet.

It's strange that along with so many important issues in life such as money, sex, and marriage, pleasure has no classroom. As I mentioned in the Introduction, I've been fortunate enough to earn four degrees—two of which are in counseling—yet I haven't taken a single course on pleasure! Imagine going your entire life without ever stopping to examine your pleasure zones.

Pleasure is so important to all of our lives . . . yet we rarely, if ever, take a moment to really understand, appreciate, and plan for it. Oh, occasionally you might mention a particular area of enjoyment in your life, but when was the last time you actually spoke in depth about your pleasures?

Most of us wouldn't even know whom to talk with about this subject matter. Is this a spiritual conversation—one we'd discuss with our pastor, therapist, or maybe our hairdresser? It's overwhelmingly odd that so much of who we are revolves around pleasure, but there's so little talk about it and no language for communicating our primary pleasure zones.

As you begin to delve into this book, you'll go where few people have traveled before—to the pleasure zones. As you flip each page, you'll go deeper into the caverns of your pleasures. You'll walk out with a plan for consistent enjoyment over the next few weeks . . . and for the rest of your life.

As with any subject, we need to start somewhere, so let's begin with the basics. In this chapter (and in Chapters 2 and 3), we're going to discuss the various pleasures. This section is important because you'll need to understand what they are as you begin to map out your own pleasure zones in future chapters.

Now, as I walk you through each of the various zones, know that only some of them will apply to you. Others will be relevant to your spouse, children, or friends. So if you come across a pleasure that's not exactly "you," keep reading, because it may help you learn how to give pleasure to someone you care about, or at least further your understanding of those you like or love.

Having been a counselor for more than 18 years, I've found it absolutely amazing how couples balance each other's often opposite, complex, and varied pleasure zones. Then when you add those wonderful creatures called children, even more variations emerge. So understanding your own zones and those of others can also help you in your marriage, with your family and friends, and even in your co-worker relationships. The application of your understanding of pleasure zones is as limitless as the relationships themselves.

In order to have this conversation on pleasure, we'll break our discussion down into three major categories—body, soul, and spirit pleasures—the first of which is the subject of this chapter. (And yes, you *will* have multiple pleasures in multiple categories . . . that's the fun of discovering your pleasure zones.)

The body pleasures are those that mostly involve your senses. As we discuss them, you'll be able to see that any one can appear in many varied forms. Two people can both have the same primary sensory pleasure, but with extremely different applications of it, so just because you and your significant other share a primary pleasure zone, you may enjoy it in two completely different ways. How you apply what you learn about any of these pleasures may vary from how others do so—that variation is what makes you wonderfully unique. Although we all may be pleasure machines, each one of us is as different as a snowflake.

Sight

There isn't a soul with the power of sight who hasn't enjoyed visual pleasure. The sheer delight of watching a sunset or a child play, the beauty of architecture, and the awesome attractiveness of the opposite sex are all visual pleasures.

I live in Colorado Springs, and every day I wake up and look at Pikes Peak . . . it's visual candy. If I want another feast for the eyes, I can go down the street from my office to the Garden of the Gods and walk around those amazing rock formations.

In my yard, I can see my children playing, which is a pleasure all by itself. Then there's the sight of my Afghan hound, Moses, running full speed, which is like watching a beautiful wild animal daily. But the most beautiful sight I encounter is the eyes, body, and face of my bride of 20 years, Lisa—a real visual pleasure.

The potential for visual pleasure is everywhere—from sea to shining sea—in the form of creatures, plants, and an endless array of fellow people on the planet. If all that weren't enough, we have our own human-made beauty, which provides many ways to visually pleasure ourselves. Who among us hasn't gotten so lost in a movie that we almost forgot we were alive?

Lisa and I recently saw a couple of films that were amazingly full of visual pleasures. The first was *King Kong.* The computer imaging of the gorilla was so well captured and believable—his hair was moving in the breeze, and his eyes showed pain as he was being bitten by the Tyrannosaurus rex. The other movie that had tremendous scenery and special effects was the film adaptation of the classic *The Chronicles of Narnia: The Lion, the Witch and the Wardrobe,* which contained grand scenes and the most believable centaur (half-man, half-horse) creature that I've ever seen. Our culture is full of sources of visual pleasure, from the Internet to cell phones.

Visual enjoyment is important to all of us to some degree, but for many it's a greater or primary pleasure. Some people will watch the sun go down, observe a wild animal for hours, or just look on with amazement at the art involved in the petals of a flower coming into bloom. They take the time to really *see* their world. For those people who have this primary pleasure zone, seeing is the well from which they drink their happiness. The sight of whatever captures their heart creates pleasure for them because they enjoy it more than most. These individuals can become great astronomers, photographers, and movie or sports critics; and they often have hobbies that reflect their need for visual pleasuring.

People who bird-watch for hours and check off what they've seen on a list could easily have a visual primary sensory-pleasure zone. The same goes for men or women who have to check if their kids are in bed and love to regularly behold the pure beauty of their sleeping children.

Touch

The sensory pleasure of touch is one that most of us have enjoyed from time to time in various forms: the hug of a friend, a caress from a loved one, snuggling with a spouse, and petting a dog or cat. This pleasure zone involves the largest organ of the body—the skin.

From head to toe, your skin covers you with endless nerves that can receive the pleasure of touch. I love touch—I mean, I really *love* it. To me, the work of a skilled massage therapist is incredible. I find that as people who are trained in this art warm up, they touch your skin and prep it for greater pleasure. I appreciate a firm massage: the deeper into my muscles, the better. To a point, I think that the masseuse is not only touching my body, but my soul as well. For those of you who drink your pleasure through touch, you know exactly what I mean. But touch can go way beyond receiving a massage.

I know people who love to play with dirt. Weekend gardeners who dig and plant with their hands often cherish the feel of the soil between their fingers. People who cook with their hands, mixing the egg salad together without the aid of a utensil, are likewise drinking in the pleasure of touch.

Most of us know people who can sit on their sofa and pet their dog or cat for hours. I'm absolutely certain that Moses has touch as *his* primary sensory zone. When Daddy (that's me) comes home, this very large dog will sit down right in front of me and wait for me to rub him down—he assumes the position to be touched. He wants more than a pat on the head and a "good doggie" . . . he wants a deep caress of his back and shoulders. He won't let me continue on my journey through the house until the needs of his primary sensory-pleasure zone are met adequately.

Now touch is different for everyone. Some mostly prefer to receive it; others by and large want to give it. A few people like both equally because to them either activity is pleasurable.

If touch is your primary sensory-pleasure zone, this is a real need. What I mean is that it isn't just a "want," although those for whom it isn't a primary pleasure may think that it is. Oh no, if your primary pleasure is touch and you aren't in physical contact with others, you get a little weird. After a good touching (given or received), it's as if the planets line up all over again, and you're ready to "do" life.

Taste

For some of you, taste is the big enchilada. I mean, who really hasn't received pleasure from some form of food? It's such a large part of our everyday experience. Like you, I love taste—I relish different flavors, sauces, and seasonings. Someone once said that variety is the spice of life. Well, when it comes to food, I'd be inclined to agree. How many of us have enjoyed a steak, seafood, or a vegetable dish that's cooked with a different twist?

Oh, I could go on and on, but I certainly can't neglect to talk about sweets. I don't know who invented baking, but my oh my, whoever it was is special to all of us. How many pies, cakes, puddings, and candies have we pleasured ourselves with over the years? Who doesn't love that season between Thanksgiving and New Year's when the stream of desserts is as steady as the brooks of Colorado? At the office, at home, and while visiting others . . . sweets are everywhere. It tastes like heaven all day long.

And we haven't even started to talk about the taste pleasure of drinking, which includes exotic coffees, teas, hot chocolates, juices, fruit smoothies, milk shakes, and other endlessly creative approaches to stimulating the palate. Oh yes, and what about all those sodas? I actually have a close friend who thinks that Mountain Dew is the nectar of the gods. Billions of dollars are spent on selling, marketing, and purchasing taste pleasures.

I can't go one step further without discussing one of the kings of taste pleasures—chocolate. There are endless forms in which to experience this treat. I must admit that I'm a fan here. One of my favorite ways to pleasure myself for a brief moment is to take a small piece of really good chocolate (not the cheap stuff), place it delicately in my mouth, and savor the sweet flavor. Not biting into it, but relishing it is how I like to experience this pleasure . . . all of you chocolate aficionados know what I mean. If taste isn't a primary pleasure zone for you, you may have no idea what I'm talking about here, and that's okay; we'll connect on one of the other pleasures.

Now the people whose primary pleasure zone is taste rarely understand those who don't really experience it in this way, and vice versa. Trust me, there are folks whose primary pleasure *isn't* taste. They can't fathom why we go on and on about a sauce or flavor for minutes and disturb their otherwise-quiet meal.

I have a friend who doesn't like sweets at all. He can't be tempted to sample cake, pie, candy, or sugary soda. He has no real taste pleasure zone. I'm married to such a person, too. Lisa enjoys ordinary foods as much as delicacies. White bread is as good as a gourmet raisin loaf. The sauces at a five-star restaurant are "good" and "okay," but never "the most magnificent combinations of texture and taste," as I might experience them. That's fine . . . she has other pleasure zones, but I say this to those who do have the primary pleasure zone of taste: Be patient and accepting when others don't want to clap with you over that piece of something spectacular that you just experienced.

Hearing

The fourth sensory pleasure we want to discuss is hearing, which runs in both directions (that is, hearing others and being heard oneself). For some, sound is an incredibly pleasurable experience. These people love to listen to concerts, classical music, jazz, nature sounds . . . almost anything.

Audio-sensory-pleasure people have a "palate" much like that of taste-sensory individuals. They need to experience some form of sound—even if it's silence, they can hear it.

Most of us know at least one audio-sensory person. They're the folks with the really expensive stereo equipment. Although some of us can't appreciate the distinction between a hundred-dollar and a thousand-dollar speaker system, to them it's the difference between life and death.

A jazz or classical concert is akin to a fine delicacy. Like the massage, it starts off slowly, but before you know it, the music has you captivated. You actually hear it touching every cell of your body. You feel the waves, the tempos, and the integrations of sound. It's almost as if your soul is going to burst right there. If you're a fan, you know what I'm talking about. If not . . . well, now you understand "them" better.

Audio-sensory pleasure also runs in the direction of giving sound. For some people, it's through music—they're the ones with their instrument in tow. They give music away as if they're bestowing their soul on others. From the classically trained to the gospel singer, from the rhythm-and-blues to the scat-jazz musician, they feel pleasure as they offer up their gift to others. Who hasn't been struck by how such individuals seem as if they were giving their hearts away in their performance. It stirs us all, and for some of us, it deeply impacts our soul in a pleasurable manner.

Audio-sensory pleasure also comes in the form of giving and receiving words. Some people derive real joy from hearing others talk. They're amazed and deeply moved by a great communicator. They create the word pictures and empathetically feel the message and meaning on more than just a verbal or content level; they really "get" what the speaker is saying.

Likewise, there are those who love to create sounds and words. These people enjoy hearing themselves talk. They like listening to their voice in the form of words, sounds, or random thinking out loud . . . they enjoy communicating. To them, the *art* of the conversation can be as important as the content. The pronouns and adjectives dance for these communicators, and telling a story—whether it's heard by anyone or not—is almost orgasmic. A joke can be heaven on earth to a word giver. Such people aren't necessarily narcissistic or self-absorbed (although others may think that they are); they just feel

9

the auditory pleasure of hearing themselves and others. They gain satisfaction from conversation.

Rarely will the audio-sensory-pleasure person understand the quiet or wise soul. They challenge others to come out and play with words—they almost taunt them, luring them into word painting.

This sensory-pleasure path needs to be celebrated just like all the others. Again, as you understand the various avenues to pleasure, you also have the opportunity to appreciate a path that isn't your primary one with those who might enjoy it more fully.

So the next time you're in an airport and you see someone with $300 Bose headphones and an accompanying CD player or iPod, don't sneer in a condescending manner, but rather acknowledge that you're in the presence of an "audio" person. Just be aware that this individual might be quite the talker once he or she has been pleasured with sound!

Smell

The last of our sensory-pleasure zones is smell. Oh, the aroma! For some of us, smells are deeply enjoyable. We inhale the scent of flowers as if we were just drinking in the flavor—just like a massage, this activity touches our soul.

When you contemplate the billions of dollars spent on smells, it's amazing. Just think of all the perfumes, antiperspirants, hair sprays, shampoos, air fresheners, car deodorizers, and different kinds of incense; and entire stores dedicated to scented candles.

Aromas are everywhere. Some people really derive more pleasure from fragrances than others, but *everybody* loves the smell of the meal and the desserts when Grandma cooks. It's as if you can taste every last trace of them in the house.

People for whom smell is a primary sensory pleasure love to inhale their food, their environment, and even the individuals around them (yes, human beings have scents, and aroma-sensory-pleasure people can breathe them in as well as hear and see them). Of course, if you're not a fan, you won't understand that very well.

I know that all the ladies who work in my counseling office love aromas. It's not uncommon for three or more candles to be burning all day long—even the lobby gets its own scent. And not just any fragrance will do. Oh no, these have to be special candles that are shipped in. When they come in to the office, it's an aroma frenzy: "Smell this one," "Ooh," and "Ah" are sounds that can be heard coming from the female employees. They drool over these candles as if they were newborn babies: No two scents are alike, and all are wonderful.

My office would be an aroma sensory-pleasure person's dream. Such people can't walk by a perfume, bath, or candle shop or the cologne area of a department store without stopping for a whiff. And you won't just hear, "Oh, that's an interesting scent"—no, no. Those pleasured by smell will say, "That's *incredible*—sniff this one, honey!" They not only want everyone else to enjoy what they're experiencing, but they also want them to enjoy it just as deeply. Aroma-sensory people become lit up like a Christmas tree as they talk you into another fragrant purchase.

These sensory-pleasure zones are all familiar to us. Even by just reading about them so far, you've probably already gained insight into yourself and a few other people of your acquaintance. I know because *I* laugh as I go through these various sensory-pleasure zones and think of some of the individuals in my life. Yet if we stopped the conversation here, we'd definitely be shortchanging ourselves.

As human beings, we are body, soul, *and* spirit, so we must continue to dialogue about the other pleasures we can experience. For some of us, it's the other two areas—*soul* and *spirit*—that really hold our primary pleasure zone.

Chapter Two

Soul Pleasures

The soul is an amazing place to receive pleasure. It's the location of our mind, will, and emotions. To say that the soul is less complex than the body is only an indication that one has never experienced its full potential. As a counselor, I witness the wonders, complexities, and resourcefulness of the soul every day at the office. The soul is a great terrain for pleasure because, much like the body, that's what it was created for.

As I've already noted, bodily or sensory pleasures vary from person to person. The same is true for the soul: Every soul experiences pleasure differently. Again, there isn't necessarily a right or wrong way—it's more about gaining an understanding of what's true for you in order to create a personal pleasure map for yourself. Doing so will also help you be more open to those around you who are wired for pleasure quite differently.

So let's start off our discussion with some primary pleasures of the soul.

Humor

We all enjoy a good laugh because it makes us feel great. A really funny joke can be as mood altering as a double cappuccino. Laughter makes the soul, body, and spirit feel uplifted. Can you remember a time while you were growing up when a sibling (or maybe even a parent) acted silly? Do you recall how it was as if you were intoxicated with humor? No matter what either of you said, you'd continue to laugh and laugh. Honestly, if others had walked in, they would have thought you were on laughing gas.

Humor can be a primary pleasure zone. For my soul, the invention of comedy CDs and DVDs is as sweet as any candy. I'll never forget the records of Steve Martin: I'd play them over and over again and chuckle at his performances. And who could forget some of Bill Cosby's memorable comedy routines? Remember Art Linkletter's television show about kids saying the darnedest things? I recall laughing so hard it hurt while listening to what children would say to Art during his show.

My kids and I love to laugh. Just yesterday my daughter, Hadassah; my son, Jubal; and I laughed hysterically after I defeated Hadassah in a game of tic-tac-toe while we were sitting in a restaurant.

Hadassah declared, "I can beat Daddy!" Now she's my oldest, and like many firstborn children, she has that attitude of being . . . well, let's say "older." We drew our tic-tac-toe board, and I went first, placing my X in the right-hand corner. Hadassah then drew another X just below mine, at which point I put a third one under hers to win the game. She suddenly realized her mistake of writing an X instead of an O in her spot, and we all laughed uncontrollably.

Humor is a great pleasure zone. For some people, it's even a primary one. I had a friend in Texas who regularly posted jokes around his office. This same man had a ritual that before he and his family had dinner, they'd read something out of one his many joke books.

Like those with other primary pleasure zones, such people love to share their enjoyment. They're the friends in your group who can always find the funny side of life, the ones who know many more jokes than you do. So get ready to laugh if you're in a relationship with one of these individuals!

Risk

The thrill of danger for a risk-pleasure-zone person reaches a zenith. Extreme-sports enthusiasts, including snow- and skateboarders, skydivers, and bungee jumpers, would definitely fall into this category. These "crazy" people aren't *really* crazy . . . they just have a primary risk/excitement pleasure zone.

These individuals actually enjoy putting their lives in danger as they're mountain biking down a ten-foot boulder. Such men and women (yes, some females have high risk/excitement pleasure zones) really get a charge out of it. Their body flows with adrenaline, and their brain chemistry is almost euphoric, but it goes much deeper than this: Their soul, mind, will, and emotions are fully engaged. They're hyperalert—receiving and interpreting information at such a high rate that they act like a supercomputer.

Those whose primary pleasure zone is risk and excitement live for adventure. Whether they're backpacking up steep mountains, scuba diving, feeding the sharks, or white-water rafting through the rivers of Africa, these people deserve and need to be celebrated. Often they travel in packs with other individuals for whom "risk/ excitement" is their primary pleasure.

If you're one of these people, you'll often feel misunderstood, and those with a different primary pleasure

15

zone may frequently question your judgment. These detractors call themselves "rational" or "normal" and use other obscure words. Don't worry—just accept that you won't be fully understood by them.

Now if you're not a risk/excitement-pleasure-zone person but you're in a close romantic or marital relationship with one, honor this fact. Ask your loved one questions, and withhold judgment about his or her seemingly insane risk taking so that he or she feels respected. As with all people who have a pleasure zone you don't share, it's much more valuable to offer patience and celebration than judgment and criticism.

Risk/excitement is a legitimate pleasure zone. I've counseled countless men who "used to" do one thing or another that met this need before they got married, became "civilized," had children, and began working a lot. Without realizing it, they eventually lost the risk and excitement in their life. They gradually got in a funk, gained weight, and even became depressed. For many men, risk, excitement, and adventure is a necessary pleasure zone, which (like all others) needs to be managed or scheduled in.

Remember that if risk is your primary soul pleasure zone, this is the well from which you drink. It's as satisfying to your soul as any sensory experience you could have.

Calm

Now let's jump to the other pleasure-zone extreme— calm. Almost nothing is more invigorating and refreshing than a strong cup of calm for those with this primary pleasure zone. I mean a really relaxing calm, such as sitting idly in a rowboat at 5 A.M. and just breathing in the surrounding mountains, the quiet of the water, the slow-moving mist, and the occasional fish that comes up to the surface.

Some of you are looking for that boat right now. Or you might enjoy lounging in a hammock, sitting on a porch, or being still almost anywhere. There's an incredible peace that comes into your being and blows the dust from the day right out of your soul . . . it's as if you can breathe again and reengage in day-to-day life.

Calm is indescribable to those wired with this primary pleasure zone. They often seek a time during the day—morning or night—that's theirs alone. They're frequently misunderstood unless they're married to, or are in a relationship with, another calm individual. Think of the couple you know who live far from the city and who've had the same neighbors for 50 years.

Calm is good—it's a legitimate pleasure zone. People who enjoy it aren't loners; rather, they simply receive pleasure in the stillness. To calm-pleasure-zone people, a good book or a quiet room in the house is heaven on earth. They seek out the calm within the storm. They don't mind working hard raising families . . . they just want tranquility somewhere along the way.

Now these individuals might be misinterpreted or even judged negatively by the risk/excitement person, but acceptance of calm individuals is important. Asking them what they experienced or thought about during their quiet time is a great way to be supportive.

17

Spending

There are some individuals whose primary pleasure is spending money . . . now here's a pleasure of the soul that can be extremely fun! Such people really love the whole process and receive pleasure from conceptualizing something to buy. Many with this pleasure zone get enjoyment out of the search for the perfect product, while others find it in the pursuit of the best deal.

Yes, to those with this primary pleasure zone, TV home-shopping channels and eBay are like the wind blowing through their hair while riding a Harley-Davidson motorcycle. The sight of the word *sale* is akin to seeing the Grand Canyon or some other wonder of the world.

Now, as with all pleasure zones, there can be extremes on both sides, but I just want to highlight the fact that spending is truly a legitimate pleasure zone. The stop at Starbucks for a $4 coffee is an escape into this zone. Shopping just for shopping's sake—you know, that casual two-and-a-half-hour stroll around the mall or outlet stores without buying anything—can be pleasurable (really!). If you aren't a spending-pleasure-zone person, much of this isn't going to make sense to you.

Like the other zones, the spending pleasure zone needs to be managed. A day here and there for shopping, or even for buying necessities, should be planned in advance. Again, there's no shame in enjoying this activity as long as debt isn't an ongoing part of the process. And if you're in a relationship with a spender, remember to ask questions about his or her excursions: What is he or she thinking about purchasing? How is the research going? How close is he or she to saving up for the item? When is a good time to look at it?

You aren't going to change the zone of others . . . it's in their DNA. So join in their joy, balancing and celebrating the different pleasure zones of the soul.

Travel

Seeing the sights, hearing the silence or the special sounds (whether they're quiet or loud), and going where no man or woman has gone before . . . travel is to this soul what a smorgasbord is to the palate.

Travel-pleasure-zone people view cities, states, countries, and continents as different foods to be consumed. They can deeply experience a river or mountain, and they're at home in the tropics of Africa—it's about their soul being out there among the sights and sounds of the world. They revel in the different, the uncommon, and the unique.

Such people find pleasure in every aspect of this process. Getting a travel idea is like meeting someone they want to date. They enjoy setting up the itinerary, packing, going to the airport, or driving down the various highways. To them, the arrival is orgasmic, and the exploring is the afterglow.

People for whom travel is a true primary pleasure zone *live* to travel, and they work so that they can save up for it. I'll never forget a couple I met who were both examples of this. The husband worked as a consultant six months at a time and drove an older car. Then he'd stop working, and he and his wife would board their very expensive boat in Mexico and sail the seas together. They were definitely in heaven half the year, and during the other half they just looked forward to the boat season. Rarely have I found two travel-pleasure-zone people so perfectly matched.

If you're such a person, you may feel stifled by having to focus on the responsibilities of life instead of the pleasures of experiencing something new. However, the needs of the travel pleasure zone may be met in smaller doses than a global voyage. You can explore where you live, but expect to want to get out of town quite a bit—whether to a lake, the mountains, or the beach.

If you yourself aren't a "travel" person, enjoy the pleasure of these activities with those who are, and they'll tend to join you in the mundane routine of daily living. Allowing others their pleasure is critical for understanding those you love. So if you're a travel-pleasure-zone person, celebrate those who aren't. They aren't boring, cheap, uncreative, or stick-in-the-muds. They just have a different hierarchy of pleasure that needs to be honored by you.

Integrity

Although it often doesn't get the airtime that some of the other zones receive, integrity is an authentic pleasure zone. There are people who really get pleasure out of doing what's right. They enjoy the fact that they don't lie, cheat, exaggerate, or try to misrepresent or harm others in any way.

They love the fact that when life offers them tricky circumstances, they choose the ethical path. They like the feeling of self-esteem they get from knowing that they have no shadows, secrets, or desires to create any strife in their lives. They love the pleasure of feeling clean on the inside. It's not something they brag about or even think much about, but they experience pleasure from doing right.

These integrity-pleasure-zone people aren't always even spiritual, although many are. They just like the feeling of doing a good job and knowing they haven't ripped anybody off. They're keenly attuned to the rhythm of life. They intuitively know and live by the golden rule of treating others as they'd want to be treated. For these integrity-pleasure-zone people, life isn't about a spirit of being showy or needing more attention than the equally valuable soul next to them.

To know an integrity-pleasure-zone person is to smell the sweet fragrance of life. They may remind you of the good in the world and within all of us.

I travel a lot to speak at conferences, where I meet a variety of people, including front-desk attendants, rental-car clerks, and hotel personnel, along with my host and colleagues. Along that journey from my house in Colorado to the podium, I often experience a couple of integrity-primary-pleasure-zone people.

These individuals invigorate me during my travels. They often go above and beyond the call of duty, and I feel cared for and special. Oh, how I love these people! Although most of us feel positive when we do good, these amazingly designed souls experience this pleasure as a regular stream in their life.

Now if you're in a primary relationship with such a person, he or she will constantly challenge your character and your decision-making process. Most of us are slightly more self-serving in our choices than integrity-pleasure-zone people, who don't ask, *What's best for me?* but rather, *What's right, fair, and equitable?* Their integrity can be frustrating if this isn't your primary pleasure zone.

If you try to go against them and manipulate them to a point of compromise, it truly hurts them deeply on a soul level. A better path is to respect their integrity . . . they love to feel good in this way. Awareness that this is their source of pleasure is critical to celebrating such individuals. When they feel your support for their pleasure, they'll return the favor.

Giving

Giving is a great delight to those who occupy this pleasure zone. Their giving doesn't stem from a sense of duty, which is no pleasure at all, but rather originates directly from the depths of the heart.

They love to give to their significant other in so many ways, offering up their time, touch, praise, and lots of little surprise gifts. They actually get pleasure from the idea of giving—from the point of the conception—much like the travel-pleasure-zone person.

From the moment they think of how to give to their spouse, child, neighbor, or friend, they feel pleasure. From that point forward, they feel pleasure every step of the way: during the phone calls to make it happen, as they're purchasing the gift, and even while writing the note to surprise the recipient.

They don't even have to see the person's face—they just feel good knowing that they did something to brighten up his or her day. For individuals with this primary pleasure zone, it's not about the size of the gift, but about the act of giving. Givers feel pleasure in dropping a compliment that encourages a store clerk; they enjoy helping a mother who's struggling to carry her child along with her bag onto a flight.

In truth, givers usually also find some broader outlet for their generosity. I know of a unique couple who both have this primary pleasure zone. Fortunately, they've done well financially and are constantly making contributions to causes they believe in. And I don't just mean little donations—I'm talking about sometimes hundreds of thousands of dollars. One of them loves to give to causes related to the nation of Israel; the other enjoys helping those in India. They don't tell you about their gifts, but they always have someone in need (often from another country) in their life or staying in their home.

The givers' joy is in releasing something that they have to another. Doing so is as delightful to them as a piece of chocolate is to a taste-pleasure-zone person. Givers have to give—that's how they feel pleasure. If you're married to one, you're fortunate when that thoughtfulness is aimed at you. When the target shifts to others, at times you may feel left behind. Understand that giving pleasure is important, but remember that givers also need to be *given to* as well. Often they can take care of others and not themselves. They also need to occasionally be on the receiving end of their own care and that of others.

Sex

Well, finally we're going to talk about sex. Yes, sex is a pleasure zone for almost all of us. I placed it in the realm of the soul, but it's really a three-dimensional pleasure, involving the spirit, soul, *and* body.

Many people focus on just the physical enjoyment of sex and miss the greater depths of pleasure that come into play when you add the soul and spirit. However, most adults know the difference between having sex and making love or being made love to by someone else. When a mature couple learns to bring all of themselves into the bedroom, it can be a pleasure that's absolutely intoxicating and bonding. Now, I'm not talking about having sex more often or trying to figure out another location or position to have it in. Beyond the physiology of sex is a place of solace for the soul and spirit to be together as one.

Here again, the person whose primary pleasure zone is sex receives gratification in the conception, the pursuit, and the act. Whether given or received (or both), acts of sex are extremely pleasurable to such an individual. In a relationship with a sexual-pleasure-zone person, understanding and celebrating this zone together is critical, as denying or mismanaging it can create great internal conflict.

Relationships

Most of us like having friends, but for some of us, our primary soul pleasure zone is interpersonal relationships. Such individuals love people: They love to be with them, to talk to them, to know what's going on with them, and to concern themselves with their lives. It goes beyond just being a "people person"—relationships with others is their primary source of pleasure.

My wife, Lisa, has a friend who's a people-pleasure-zone person. This woman usually gets dozens of phone messages because she has more girlfriends than you can imagine and has called them all to see how they're doing. She'd rather connect with people than work, hang out at home, or do almost anything else. She, Lisa, and a couple of other friends get together for coffee on a regular basis. Everyone has a good time, but for this woman it's heaven: girlfriends, Starbucks, and time to enjoy both.

Those for whom relationships is a primary pleasure zone must form connections. They need time to experience and be in touch with the lives of others. If you're married to (or are in a relationship with) a people-pleasure-zone person, it can be loads of fun. You'll never run out of friends or social invitations, and you'll have plenty to talk about daily. However, spending all this time with friends and maintaining constant phone contact can be tiresome.

Honoring people with this pleasure zone is also important. When they finally get off the phone, they're recharged. Asking them about their friends is like offering candy to a taste-pleasure person. They can go on and on, but celebrate and enjoy this because it's their primary pleasure zone.

Creativity

I remember a particular scene in the movie *Chariots of Fire,* which is about a man who's training to run in the Olympics. He's being interviewed about why he races, and he says something to the effect that when he runs, he feels the pleasure of why God made him. He goes on to become a missionary after the competition.

People whose primary pleasure zone is creativity feel exactly the same pleasure as the Olympic runner when they're creating something, whether it's by cooking, writing, talking, or just thinking. To them, inventing something different or better or making something out of nothing is an incredible rush.

These creative-pleasure-zone people apply their creativity to every area of their lives. They like to regularly come up with a different workout simply to see what happens. They throw spices into ordinary food just to invent a new version of the same dish. In business, they come up with fresh ideas for doing things, as well as new products, books, movies, stories, and adventures. They just enjoy creating, whether it's sculpting a clay pot or changing the way of life for a person, community, or nation. Where would we be without those creative-pleasure people in the fields of medicine, engineering, and computers (not to mention the whizzes who came up with those amazing do-everything cell phones)?

Like individuals with other primary pleasure zones, the creative-pleasure-zone person feels the rush upon conception. The designer who conceives of a set for a theater production experiences the thrill of drawing it out on paper. What it looks like and how it moves, disappears, changes, and reappears is a total joy. The act of creating is as sensational as the impact of the nails, glue, tape, and paint when it all comes together. The creative-pleasure-zone person is delighted: The sounds of the hammers, the painters, the loud music, and the slamming of the wood on the floor are like a concert from a phenomenal orchestra.

Creative-pleasure-zone people can be quite overwhelming to be around. Change is constant, and the chaos before the creating doesn't seem to bother them; after all, they're nurturing a new "baby." That novel, system, design, business, artwork, or rearrangement of the furniture is a primary focus.

I remember someone telling me that I should read a book on Donald Trump. As I learned more about his amazing real-estate ventures, I was struck by just how creatively driven he is. Trump loves to make deals that involve a lot of creativity. He enjoys "painting" on the canvas of a major city skyline.

Creative-pleasure-zone people are all around us. They like forming ideas. Asking them a question or giving them a problem to solve can generate an answer such as "We could do things in this, that, or the other way." If you aren't a creative-pleasure-zone person, this type of response could become frustrating—especially since

26

creative types can start working on all three ideas before you can clearly and thoroughly think through one option! Being patient and enjoying the ride of "Oh, and then we could do this . . . !" is part of accepting their pleasure zone. Such people gravitate to lots of projects, problems, or opportunities like the planets orbit the sun.

Have fun with these folks, because the journey will be full of color and change. You'll constantly grow just so that you can keep up as they research this or that. Smile and encourage them even as you quietly feel inside: *Here we go again.*

❁

Arbitrarily limiting anyone's primary pleasure zone can create difficulty. Telling a travel person, "I'll only go 30 miles with you; after that, you're on your own" or saying to a touch person, "I'll only massage your back twice a year" will cause significant problems. The conflict they feel is between their need for pleasure and their relationship with you, and it can be avoided if you honor their zones.

There are many other unique pleasure zones that you might be experiencing. In the soul and sensory realms alone, I acknowledge that there could be specific things that you would have liked to have seen mentioned here. Therefore, before we move on to *spiritual* pleasure zones, I thought you might want to take a moment to jot down any particular pleasures that apply to you while you're reflecting on them. On a separate piece of paper or in a journal, write out some of your other pleasure zones that weren't listed in these pages.

❁ ❁ ❁

Chapter Three

Spirit Pleasures

I want to discuss a world that many find to be a pleasure zone—the realm of the spirit. Even if you've never had any significant spiritual leanings, it's important to know about this zone for the sake of understanding other people better. The various pleasure zones are among the things that make our species amazing. As human beings, we're as different and unique among ourselves as any creature in the entire animal kingdom.

Spiritual pleasure zones are real. Billions of dollars are spent on religious development, worship centers, and organizations promoting a range of spiritual beliefs as broad as the ocean.

I want you to know that I have absolutely no ideological agenda in this chapter—that's not the purpose of the pleasure zones. I just want you to identify yet another area where you might already be receiving pleasure, or where you might consider doing so.

Meditation

There's an absolute joy in meditation: Your mind is clear, your body is calm, and the only things moving are your heart and lungs. When you're at peace, it's as if you can feel the world slowly move within your own stillness.

Meditation is sweet, intoxicating, and "wowing" to those for whom it's a primary pleasure zone. In fact, I know a woman who has a special room in her house just for this activity. She assumes a comfortable position, and all of life stops around her. She exists within the silence of her wonderful self.

For some people, meditation is an absolutely cleansing phenomenon, in which they block out all thoughts and just purge themselves of the world around them. In that moment, they're as focused as a downhill skier or mountain biker . . . totally lost in the moment.

Others practice a form of meditation that may include thoughts or music. They also get in a comfortable position, but they focus on an idea, spiritual thought, or world issue. They meditate as a way to achieve clarity about what's on their mind. They might use their back porch, a hammock, or a quiet space anywhere.

Some people intentionally utilize meditation in their lives for the sake of others, although they wouldn't necessarily call it by that name. I know a man who slips off to his hammock in the backyard when he comes home from work. Before engaging in all the joys of parenting, marriage, and housework, he lies there for 15 to 30 minutes just feeling the hammock's slow movements and experiencing relaxation. He's then refreshed and able to give more of himself to his family. He doesn't refer to this as "meditation"—he calls it "escaping"—but he enjoys it like a cold drink on a summer's day.

I regularly see some of these meditators on the plane. They have their headsets on and are off in a place of tranquility. They aren't sleeping; rather, they're connecting to a meditative state.

If you're someone whose primary pleasure zone is meditation, you'll need to meet this need quite regularly. It's the way you experience pleasure and feel centered in your immediate surroundings and the world at large. To those of you in a primary relationship with such a person, celebrate these moments of aloneness that give your loved one the recharging he or she needs in order to be a good partner and face the demands of life.

Prayer

Prayer is a pleasure zone that's distinct from meditation, since it's a talking-aloud and active-listening process. Prayer, unlike meditation, has a deity focus—something that's unique to this pleasure.

Prayer is based on either a spiritual or a religious belief in a higher power. Now these distinctions are important:

— A **spiritual** belief in a deity is relational; that is, there's some interaction between the deity and the one who's praying. It's an offering or a communication of the self to the divine. The two beings are friends who are in an unequal relationship. It's like having an uncle, grandfather, or mother who loves you for who you are but who can see the unrefined spots in your life and has the resources to support your growth.

— A **religious** belief involves more of an object relationship with a deity. Often this supreme being has the ability to help but must first be pleased by a special performance or a litany of statements, and religious people are often more formal in the way they approach the higher power. The pleasure is in checking off the box or doing a "right" spiritual act, as opposed to engaging in a relationship.

Praying can be extremely pleasurable. Opening your heart to the divine can be incredibly engaging, cleansing, and empowering.

Praying for others, whether they're strangers or people you know well, can also be a wonderful experience for those who have this pleasure zone. I know some people who call themselves *intercessors*. They receive real joy in pouring their hearts out on behalf of others. When they're done, they report experiencing intense pleasure spiritually, emotionally, and physically.

Prayer-pleasure-zone people need sufficient time to pursue their pleasure. Their praying allows them to feel connected to their deity as well as to those around them. They feel awesome knowing that they bring those they love closer to the divine on a regular basis.

If you're in a significant relationship with—or are married to—a prayer-pleasure-zone person, engage him or her on this level. Ask questions about your partner's prayer experiences, and share your real concerns about your life so that he or she can pray for you. Doing so will make your loved one feel honored and valued.

Service

The service pleasure zone also has a religious or "cause" focus. People with this pleasure zone feel joy in advancing their spiritual beliefs or causes. The beliefs themselves aren't the issue; the pleasure they receive in advancing them is what's important.

Such people find pleasure in teaching the young, their peers, and even those outside of the fold of their faith. This may take place in a local community of similar believers or by serving in some broader manner to help get the news out about their convictions.

Often "servers" won't just stop at donating their personal time but will often contribute financially as well. They work hard and give a percentage of their income to forward their cause locally, nationally, or globally.

They feel pleasure when serving and have a need to be a part of something bigger than themselves. They really like volunteering for service within their belief structure. Again, if you're in a relationship with a server, celebrate this fact. Your loved one will set aside time and money to serve, but afterward he or she is usually charged up about life and his or her relationship with you.

u

You've been exposed to so many pleasure zones, and yes, you'll usually have more than one. Finding and managing them will be the focus of future chapters. For right now, you might just want to pause for a moment and reflect on the idea that you're a being who's made for pleasure. You're uniquely created for a combination of pleasure zones that are yours and yours alone. Nobody you know has the exact pleasure-zone hierarchy that you do.

There's joy in discovering the special value of your own pleasure zones and in honoring and appreciating those of the people around you. Believe me, as you get good at detecting pleasure zones, you'll be able to identify them in your friends, children, parents, co-workers, and partner.

Once you uncover the zones of others, you'll find yourself engaging in more positive, supportive conversations with those whose zones are different from your own. The golfer and the skydiver can support each other on any given day as they both individually express their own respective pleasure zones.

I hope that you're enjoying identifying primary pleasure zones, and I heartily welcome you to the pleasure-zone lifestyle!

❦ ❦ ❦

Chapter Four

The Power of Pleasure

Pleasure is often an unseen force that makes things happen. That it's invisible doesn't in any way mitigate the fact that there's real power involved. By way of analogy, let's talk about a couple of other unseen powers that you encounter regularly in your daily life.

You can feel the wind at times, and you can hear it on some days as well. There are few things that feel better than a cool breeze on a beach or in the mountains. Yet the wind is absolutely unseen. You can, however, witness its impact and even harness its great power. I know that many of us were amazed by a pinwheel for at least a few moments during our childhood. We would watch this almost flower-shaped object that by itself wasn't all that engaging. Then the wind would come along and catch it, and the pinwheel would spin and spin. The harder the wind blew, the faster the little pinwheel would work.

Humankind has made greater applications of the pinwheel in modern times. The unseen power of the air moves large windmills, creating enough energy to power a house or even entire neighborhoods if it's used intelligently. Gravity is another unseen "stealth" power. You meet with this force on a daily basis. Every time you put yourself on the scale, you experience its power. As you walk, play, or throw things, gravity is in place—it's a real power, and you never win when you come into conflict with it. Like the wind, gravity is unseen but has an important place in your life. . . .

I could go on and on about the effects of the many unseen powers that are around us every day, but I think you get the point.

Pleasure is one of these very significant powers. You can't see it, but you can recognize its impact. What pushes a person to run, swim, eat sweets, shop, or meditate? . . . It's pleasure that motivates these behaviors. You can't observe it with your eyes, but its power can be one of the largest influences in your life and in the lives of those you love.

The power of pleasure is at work daily—it's consistently but invisibly in your life. It drives you at times but can't be perceived directly. It helps you make both major and minor decisions about how you spend your time, energy, and money. Occasionally, the power of pleasure also dictates your choice of relationships.

You see, your life is like that pinwheel: There's an invisible wind propelling you. As you continue to read, your eyes may open to seeing the power of pleasure in your life. You'll come to look upon it as the unseen driver of your car. You'll also be able to harness it so that you can lead a life of ongoing enjoyment. You were created for pleasure, just as the pinwheel was created for the wind.

Once you understand and harness your pleasure zones and get them to work for you, your life can be transformed. Imagine a life that's balanced and takes you from pleasure to pleasure.

Because we don't understand pleasure, we can often suffer the consequences of not managing its power, which is something one of my clients experienced. Mary was a 42-year-old television producer who was divorced and trying to raise two teenagers in a major city. Her job was very challenging: She met lots of different people every week and talked on the phone for hours a day. In addition, she had to deal with her ex-husband, boyfriend, and children and still try to stay in shape.

When introduced to the pleasure-zone theory, Mary was sure she had a "doughnut and coffee" pleasure zone. Of course, she was half-kidding. Mary really had a private battle with burnout, being angry with her children, and generally feeling fatigued. These are classic symptoms of living outside of one's pleasure zone.

In talking to Mary, I asked her when she'd felt more balanced and happy in life. Surprisingly, she said that she'd felt this way when she was married. Even though her ex-husband was intolerable and immature, he always used to rub her back for 10 to 30 minutes a night. He'd sometimes massage her deeply and other times scratch or lightly touch her. Regardless, this physical contact deeply recharged her, as her primary sensory-pleasure zone was touch.

Since she'd gotten divorced, the touching had disappeared. She didn't let her new boyfriend give her a massage because it was too early in the relationship and she didn't trust him entirely yet. So Mary went over her schedule to see when she had free time. She realized that since she worked late on Thursdays, she didn't have to go in to work on Fridays until noon. She made a plan to have a deep-tissue massage every Friday morning for six weeks to see if indulging her pleasure zone of touch would make a difference in her life. She found a very safe, skilled massage therapist, and it didn't even take Mary the whole six weeks to find her life more in balance and to begin to feel better and more relaxed at work and home. She liked her therapist so much that she made a six-month commitment, agreeing to pay for the services even if she didn't show up every Friday at 9 A.M.

Mary hadn't been aware of the need for this pleasure zone in her life. When she was able to see and manage it, life became better for her and for those depending on her.

Why Should You Understand Your Pleasure Zones?

Here's the question I get asked the most: *Why should I understand my pleasure zones, Dr. Doug?* Well, I want to address this early on in the book. You're about to take a journey over the next several pages as we discuss your very important pleasure zones—why should you embark on it? Let's just talk about a few of the reasons.

Relationships

We're in relationships with numerous individuals during our lives, including our spouse, parents, neighbors, friends, co-workers, acquaintances, and others we see on a semi-regular basis. Now most of us don't think about our power to make these people's lives better or worse. Actually, if we're honest with ourselves, rarely do we even contemplate how we affect them.

Yet we do. Take my clients, for example: They fly from all over the world to come see me and the team of therapists who work beside me. I impact their lives while they're with me and hopefully long after our meetings. If I'm not living in my pleasure zones, several things can happen:

- I can get resentful about being at the office.

- I can look for ways to cut things shorter
  with my clients than I need to.

- I can lack focus, which provides a poorer
  quality of service.

- My creativity can suffer, limiting solutions
  for my clients.

- I can act cross with both my clients and
  my staff.

All of this could leave the emotional environment at my office tense instead of pleasant. Even if you're smart and aware of pleasure zones, by not applying them, you can negatively affect your relationships.

Apply this notion to your home. If as a parent you're less aware or focused on your children's world, you may tolerate their existence instead of celebrating them—doing just another math-homework problem or science project. Also, as a spouse, if you're outside of your pleasure zones, you're less fun to be with or talk to.

Because you're outside your pleasure zones, you can get extremely selfish. You're less likely to be "part of the team" around the house when there are things that need to be done. You're more apt to be critical of your partner and focus on what he or she isn't doing. Most of us who've been married for a while know what it's like when our spouse is outside of their pleasure zone—and it's usually not good.

Work

Many of us are working day in and day out. When we're not in our pleasure zone, our job is definitely impacted. Meeting deadlines can seem depressing, instead of challenging and rewarding. Our "good" boss might somehow turn out to be less likable when we're out of our pleasure zone.

I know one man who was so far outside of his that he actually snapped at his boss and the other people on his team. This not only impacted his work relationships, it also got him fired!

Your ability to creatively communicate and solve problems can get also jammed. Your productivity decreases, which doesn't help the way you feel about yourself. Although there are many great reasons to embrace your unique pleasure zones, being productive and enjoying your work is a good enough one. I know that when I stay in my zone, I get more book and conference ideas. As I manage the unseen power of pleasure, my productivity goes through the roof. I know when I'm "pleasure zoning" because I'm able to keep things growing positively in my office—it's great!

Yourself

One of the best reasons to stay in your unique pleasure zone is for your own sake. You have to value and celebrate yourself regularly. You exist in a limited time and space for pleasure. When you abandon yourself and live outside your primary pleasure zones, *you* are impacted. You feel physically less vibrant and healthy, and you lose some of your perkiness. Emotionally, you're prone to becoming more pessimistic.

I think to some degree we each innately see the world more positively or negatively. My wife would rate me as a 12 on an optimism scale of 1 to 10. I love life! Problems are challenges that lead to rewards; failure is temporary, if it's real at all . . . and so on. Yet if I abandon my pleasure zones, my level of optimism drops significantly.

I begin to ask questions: *Why bother? Why push so hard? Why not sell everything and live in the mountains?* The crazy, pessimistic thoughts begin coming in because I'm living outside of my pleasure zone. My mental sharpness, wit, and humor also are impacted. I generally don't feel good about myself or my life, relationships, work, family, or projects.

Acceptance

Your pleasure zones are unique to you. I hope that by now you're at least seeing their power. You're created for pleasure, and as you realize this, it can change your life.

I know that when I accept a truth into my heart, it alters my behavior. For example, if I believed that I had a medical condition, I'd change what I needed to.

Let me tell you a true story about what happened to two good friends of mine. This husband and wife are about the biggest-hearted couple I've ever met. They've brought foster kids into their lives for over two decades. They are loving and caring people who have a couple of their own children, one of whom is named Brian.

Brian was 17 and full of life. He had good friends, was athletic, and was involved in his spiritual community. One night at 11 o'clock, I received a phone call from the couple, who frantically told me, "Brian is in the emergency room and might die—hurry down!"

41

My wife and I jumped into the car and quickly arrived at the hospital, where we found Brian's parents scared to death. Brian was almost totally blue in color. He was hooked up to practically every machine imaginable as a courageous team of doctors and nurses applied their skills trying to save his life.

Later, the doctor came out and explained that Brian had gone into diabetic shock. Now, neither Brian nor his parents knew that he'd become diabetic. He stayed in the hospital for a few days until he was stabilized. Afterward, he underwent some training about his diabetes. He was instructed about diet, exercise, and how to test his blood-sugar level.

Brian did fine for a while. However, within a couple of months, I received another phone call about his being in the hospital, almost dead again. He was eventually released and became stable . . . then he again went to the emergency room, and then once more after that.

What was Brian's problem that he kept struggling to stay alive? It wasn't that he was misinformed or unintelligent when it came to his disease. He was simply in denial—he just didn't want to be diabetic. He was 17 and not supposed to have a medical condition that demanded so much time to manage. You see, it took Brian almost an entire year to accept the new lifestyle required by his diabetes. He had to accept that he was diabetic. Once he did, his behavior changed positively.

This is true of those who have addictions as well. Before addicts of any type can change, they first have to admit: "My name is _____, and I am an addict."

Acceptance is also the key to living in one's pleasure zone. It means that I honor the fact that I have unique pleasure zones, and I recognize all the other people who have different ones. No single zone is any better than the others—just different. Acceptance means that I alone am responsible for having a plan and following it in order to stay in my pleasure zones.

One way to gain acceptance is to do a pleasure-zone history. If you examine a history of your spending patterns, you quickly become aware of what your values are. If you do a relationship or sexual history, you also learn and recognize things about yourself. In the recovery process for addiction, you similarly take a look at the history of your addiction to further help you accept it.

What I want to do here is to walk through your pleasure history—that's right, a history of how you received pleasure and were motivated by it throughout your life. What I hope to accomplish is for you to clearly figure out your unique pleasure history. Now I realize that depending on your parents' awareness of *their* pleasure zones, you may not even be conscious of some of your primary pleasure zones. The goal here is for you to see the wind that's already been moving the pinwheel of your life. Once you recognize your primary pleasure zones, you can get a step closer to integrating and maintaining them. When you have this lifestyle actively in place, you're less likely to end up in the pleasure "emergency room" and can actually have a great time living life to the fullest.

Before we start working on your pleasure history, let's just briefly review some of the primary pleasure zones. You'll need these categories to help you do your pleasure history.

Body Pleasure Zones	Soul Pleasure Zones	Spirit Pleasure Zones
Sight	Humor	Meditation
Touch	Risk	Prayer
Taste	Calm	Service
Hearing	Spending	
Smell	Travel	
	Integrity	
	Giving	
	Sex	
	Relationships	
	Creativity	

Now let's do a pleasure history. Remember that this is your unique history. I want you to just write what you think your pleasure zones were at each stage of life in four categories: *body, soul, spirit,* and *wished for.* (In the wished-for zone, it could be something you wished had been a part of your life in that age-group—be it kind words, quiet days, or horseback riding—since some of us didn't get to experience our pleasure zones as children.) Let me give you an example of what I mean for a junior-high-school-aged youth.

Age	Body Zone	Soul Zone	Spirit Zone	Wished for
12–14	Discovering new things	Relationships	Not applicable	Playing music

Walk through each stage of life and write out your pleasure history. On a separate piece of paper, fill out your body, soul, spirit, and wished-for pleasure zones for each of the following categories (up to your current age):

- Elementary school (ages 6–11)
- Junior high (ages 12–14)
- High school (ages 15–19)
- 20s
- 30s

- 40s
- 50s
- 60s+

Feel free to be creative. Because your pleasure zones are unique, don't feel limited to what I've written. Think outside of any paradigms I've discussed, and most important, try to be honest with yourself.

Now let's reflect on your pleasure zones. On a separate piece of paper or in a journal, please write what you've learned about your pleasure zones:

- What I learned about my body pleasure zones is . . .

- What I learned about my soul pleasure zones is . . .

- What I learned about my spirit pleasure zones is . . .

- What I learned about my wished-for pleasure zones is . . .

You're well on your way now to accepting your pleasure zones. It's important to bring your acceptance along with you on the journey. Without it, you won't take on the responsibility of creating a pleasure-zone lifestyle.

You deserve to read on and go for it all: acceptance, plan, and execution. I hope that you're enjoying this view of your pleasure zones and those of others so far. I promise you, as we say in Colorado, it only gets better the higher you climb!

ξ϶ ξ϶ ξ϶

Chapter Five

The Overpleasurer

Charlie was a likable guy. He lived 30 minutes out of town and worked as a plumber in his small community. His wife, Cheryl, had a job in the sheriff's department and had been there for more than 13 years.

Charlie's pleasure zone was hunting and fishing. Now Charlie wasn't just a once-in-a-while hunter or fisher—he was almost a professional. By "almost," I mean that he spent money like a professional but didn't make any, although Cheryl had to admit that the meat and fish were delicious.

Charlie had a license for almost anything you were allowed to hunt in the state. He would take off several days during the week and sometimes weeks at a time, occasionally going to other states and even to Canada to fish or hunt. Charlie was full of stories about this hunting expedition or that fishing trip.

This was all fantastic except for a few issues. Charlie and Cheryl had six children, ranging in age from 14 years old down to the littlest, who was 4. They were great kids, but Dad wasn't around most of the time, according to the family. When Charlie came back from a weeklong or more hunting or fishing excursion, he had numerous plumbing jobs to do and would end up working 16-hour days for two weeks just to catch up. He would often lose work opportunities because of his lack of availability, and he was now competing with a new plumber who'd moved into town.

Charlie and Cheryl also had financial problems, even though they lived in a small house and drove older cars. When Cheryl put together the prior year's expenses, she was shocked: Charlie had spent 57 percent of their disposable income (that is, their money after bills, clothes, and food) on his trips, including gas and hotels. She also put together a chart of his days off: If Charlie had worked half of them, they could have been in a house with more bedrooms and had a newer van to drive the children around in.

You see, Charlie is an example of someone who's overpleasuring. He was almost obsessed with his primary pleasure zone, regardless of its impact on his family or his finances.

Overpleasuring can become a problem. It's not always as extreme as Charlie's, however. Take Susan, for example. She's the sweetest woman you could ever meet. A 34-year-old from Texas, she has two children with her husband, John, who's an ob-gyn.

Susan's heart and smile are both as big as Texas. Her primary pleasure zone is giving. She's head of the PTA for the private school her children attend. Some say she's there so much that she should be one of the paid staff. She heads the fund-raisers, helps with sporting events, and goes to additional meetings at the school.

She's also involved in her church. Not only is she in the choir, but she's also part of the small women's mission group. She has two active children and puts more miles on her car than John, who lives 30 minutes from his new office. Money isn't an issue for John and Susan, but her time availability is.

John comes home to notes on the refrigerator on a regular basis: Such and such friend needed this, or the school or church had something come up. And, oh yes—her three sisters live close enough to demand her attention at any given moment. John loves Susan very much, but he rarely gets priority in her schedule.

She's often late if they plan a lunch together (which John already has limited time to enjoy), and she's tired at the end of almost every day. John wryly remarks to her, "I'd like to hear about your day, but I think that you'll be too tired to tell me all the stories."

"Stories" are right: She ran into this person, who reminded her of another friend who needed something that she forgot at home, and as she was driving there, the cell phone rang with a call from her daughter about something *she* needed. She stopped by the school at several points, and the kids had to be picked up at two different times because of their son's drama rehearsal.

For some of you this sounds normal. You might be able to identify with Susan and her life. She receives pleasure from giving. Everyone loves her and can depend on her—except her husband. John gets frustrated but is accused of being less than understanding if he says anything. She feels bad about how she neglects John regularly, forcing him to fend for himself as she leaves for another important meeting.

Susan is just as guilty of overpleasure as Charlie. Now, she didn't blow the budget, but she *is* cutting into the time she can spend with the whole family and negatively impacting her marriage with her overpleasuring.

Nine Characteristics of Overpleasurers

1. The Way They Talk

One of the most telltale earmarks of an overpleasurer is the way they talk about their enjoyment. Whatever their primary pleasure zone is becomes the topic of almost every conversation.

I find it amazing that you can often tell a person's pleasure zone by how they give directions. I can always identify a food-pleasure-zone person in this way. If you ask such an individual how to get to a school, he or she tells you: "Go about a mile and you'll see a Wendy's, then go one block farther [they don't know what's on *that* corner], turn right, and drive two miles until you pass Dunkin' Donuts. When you see Subway, make a left and you're there." Now I know it sounds extreme, but you'd be surprised by how many times I've received directions in this way.

Here's my point: Overpleasurers tend to bring the conversation back to their primary pleasure zone. You might be having a get-together and talking about anything—kids, politics, spirituality, the economy, or just life—and Joe (primary pleasure zone: *hiking*) relates it to a mountain he climbed: "Oh yeah, that reminds me of Kilimanjaro—it was so cold that I thought we were going to die." Or Alice (primary pleasure zone: *people*) might say, "Oh yeah, that reminds me of Karen, Mary, and Joan. They did the same thing about that issue, and I think they went to see Dr. Smith."

Most of us know an overpleasurer. I occasionally go to a cabin about an hour up into the mountains from Colorado Springs, where there's a great lake that's noted for its fishing. There are mostly retired people around whose primary pleasure zone is—you guessed it—fishing. Oh my, if you make any reference to the lake whatsoever, you're going to get a fishing story of some kind: "Oh yeah, three years ago I caught this pike, and it almost pulled me into the water. . . ."

I think you get the idea. As you become increasingly aware of pleasure zones, you'll be much more attuned to primary-pleasure-zone conversations. Now all of us talk about our pleasures, but overpleasurers talk about them most of the time. When you ask them questions, you'll find that this is all they want to discuss. This is because they've already worn out all of their other co-workers and friends, and you're the only one still willing to listen! So be patient with them and see if you can redirect them into another line of conversation such as work or some other unrelated topic.

2. Their Friends

Overpleasurers are rarely confronted about their over-pleasuring by their friends. You might be thinking, *Why not?* How could someone whose life is so imbalanced not be questioned about it? The answer is quite simple: Overpleasurers tend to have a small circle of friends. Not only that—it's usually a small circle of friends who have exactly the same pleasure zone, which is expressed in exactly the same way.

For example, take a group of friends who all write plays or music. They'll spend countless hours together practicing, talking, and running ideas past each other. And how about the sports-entertainment group? I remember a client came to me who would sit in front of the television all weekend watching "the games." He'd go to his friends' houses, and they'd come to his. He even recorded games that he might miss. He hung around a small group of what his wife called "sports nerds." They knew all the stats and players of various teams in several sports.

This guy was a lawyer, so he worked hard during the week and then called his buddies for the weekend plan. This went on for years and years. If his kids wanted to see Dad, they knew that he was in the basement watching TV.

In Colorado, we have rock climbing, white-water-rafting, skiing . . . all kinds of outdoor pursuits. Again, these are all great hobbies, yet whenever you go to visit the mountain towns where these activities take place and are readily available, there's usually a small group of people who live for the climb, the white water, or the ski season. Their entire circle of friends "all do it." That's the norm when you compare yourself with the other overpleasurers with whom you associate.

3. Entitlement

An overpleasurer doesn't live or see life as a balance of relationships, responsibilities, and pleasure. Pleasure moves from a place of moderation to one of prominence. It becomes more important than the duties of family, friends, community, and sometimes even work.

This out-of-balance perspective shows itself in the feeling of entitlement . . . you know, the attitude that says, "I not only have the right; I have the right—right now!" This attitude permeates the overpleasurer's primary relationships.

It doesn't even have to be the extremes of skiing or drinking with the guys or girls every weekend. Take the case of Darren—his pleasure seemed small, yet it dictated so much about the way his family related to him.

Darren's dad read the newspaper more religiously than any man alive. When he did, it was a solemn occasion for the family. If Mom wasn't home and Darren interrupted his dad for anything less than bleeding profusely, he was greeted with rage and a tirade about what an unthankful and disrespectful child he was to interrupt someone who was reading the paper.

Darren himself kept the "silent man behind the newspaper" tradition in his own family. He really received pleasure in his soul from feeling intelligent and being informed about what was going on around the world and in his community. Darren, however, developed a sense of entitlement.

At breakfast no words were spoken, and on Sunday it was hellishly quiet for about two hours until he was finished reading. Darren's entitlement was so obvious to his wife that she knew better than to talk. The children would tiptoe to get outside where they could scream, yell, and throw things.

You see, entitlement seeps into the heart of overpleasurers to the point where if you get between them and the pleasure, you pay. To them, it's as if you were saying no to life itself.

We all know people who, regardless of how sick their child or spouse is, are still going to go do such and such. I enjoy pleasure as much as the next person, but I know that I'm not entitled to it at all times over and above my relationships or responsibilities.

My pleasure plans are made with an awareness of the reality that things can change at any time. I also hold to the core belief that my life is long enough to allow any pleasure to come again. So be careful about entitlement, as it shows that you're moving toward overpleasure. I know—I don't like this red flag either, but it helps me keep my pleasure in a balance with everything else going on in my life.

4. Anger

On the heels of entitlement is another lovely little monster called anger. We all know when this little guy is in charge.

Because pleasure is the top priority, overpleasurers will sometimes bully those around them into compliance. It's the typical shaming of the person who's in the way. It doesn't seem to make any sense that a man should become angry with his daughter for getting the flu and causing him to miss a basketball game. (Don't worry, guys: Some women also get mad because their kids are sick—they, too, can't engage in whatever pleasures they'd planned.)

Now this yelling, screaming, and cursing type can be identified pretty easily. However, as a counselor, I know that not all people show their anger in the same manner.

Some overpleasurers get even. You know what I mean: Since they can't do their pleasure, they'll make certain you can't do yours either. These passive-aggressive overpleasurers aren't fun to be with at all. They show their anger by keeping score and making sure that you don't have more pleasures than they do. They think, *If I have to miss bowling, then by hook or by crook, you're not going out with your friends either—or if you do, you'll wish you hadn't!*

Another form of anger is withholding love. Some overpleasurers will be silent, ignore you, and make you say things repeatedly. This type of punishment can go on for days or weeks until you give in and let them have their way.

Anger is the signature of an overpleasurer. Their rage goes beyond disappointment and frustration . . . it reaches the next step of making someone else feel pain for their discomfort. We as adults know the difference.

5. Primary-Relationship Strain

The primary relationship of an overpleasurer is often negatively impacted. The once free, loving, adventurous relationship is less fun for the person's partner. As you might suppose, when one spouse is overpleasuring, it often takes away from the other and the family. The constant joke in an overpleasurer's family is: *Where's Mom? Oh yeah, I bet I know. She's* _____. Then they fill in the blank with whatever the overpleasurer's primary pleasure zone is.

I've counseled several couples over the years where golf was the primary pleasure zone of the husband. He might play some during the week and have regular ball-hitting practice times, but Saturday or Sunday (or both) would be a golf day. The husband would get up at 6 A.M. and be out of the door by 7. He'd have breakfast with his friends, shoot some golf, have lunch, and then sometimes go out on the green again until 6 P.M. This obviously can strain even a good marriage.

All pleasuring takes time—setting aside some for your pleasure is a good thing. *Over*pleasuring, though, usually takes a significant amount of time away from the family on a regular basis. The season is limited for some overpleasurers, such as a golfer in Colorado (it's really hard

55

to find a golf ball in the snow). However, the same golfer in Florida, California, or Arizona has almost a year-round opportunity to overpleasure.

The partners of overpleasurers begin to feel quite alone in their relationship. They feel married to their husband's or wife's pleasure zone. The left-out spouse carries most of the load of taking care of the children and other responsibilities.

The joys of marriage and the sheer miracle of parenting become burdensome. The overpleasurer focuses on the downside of these obligations, while his or her significant other feels merely tolerated.

Overpleasurers have yet to strike the balance between relationships, responsibility, and pleasure. The arguments start up about how the spouse who feels overburdened with the duties of the relationship and family has become no fun. Meanwhile, the overpleasurer is spending excessive amounts of time and sometimes resources on the pleasure activity.

You can see how the stage is set: First, it's small wisecracks, then sarcasm, then the occasional silence. In time—you guessed it—a big blowout ensues, either because the overpleasurer wants more, or because one spouse feels neglected, unimportant, or trapped by all the responsibilities, while the other gets to stay a child and play all the time.

Fun dates for the husband and wife become infrequent, and less importance is attached to them. Mutual dreams fade like an old photograph of someone you never knew. Life is no longer enjoyable for either person because the overpleasuring spouse has yet to learn balance.

This reminds me of Mike and Cassandra, an attractive couple in their mid-20s with two small children. Mike had a stable job at a local corporation. Cassandra's pleasure was music, more specifically, singing. She sang at weddings and special events as well as in her church choir.

Choir took up Wednesday, Thursday, and early Sunday mornings. Recently, Cassandra had joined a worship band, which practiced Monday, Tuesday, and some Saturdays, with gigs on Friday or Saturday night and even some Sunday evenings at coffee shops.

Cassandra always seemed to be gone, leaving Mike at home with the two boys. Mike felt neglected as his wife pursued "stardom." Her pleasure had led to many arguments before they finally came to my office. Eventually they were able to create a pleasure plan that made more sense for both of them.

6. Difficulty with Feelings

I know this may sound really funny, but difficulty with feelings is a common characteristic of an overpleasurer. I remember when I was in high school, you could always pick out the overpleasurers who used marijuana too much. These poor potheads could barely put whole sentences together. They could "yeah," "uh-huh," and "hmmm" really well, but expressing a complete thought was really difficult for them. (This was pretty amusing to watch in English class!)

I use this example because many of us knew at least a few of these kids in our high school. Although they might have been great people, their concentration was challenged.

Overpleasurers are often *emotionally* challenged. They can say "Whee, that was fun," grunt, and be angry when things don't go their way, yet to really share their array of feelings is difficult.

I've seen overpleasurers swat at the feelings of others like flies at a picnic. Problems identifying, communicating, and valuing emotions are characteristics of over-pleasurers. After all, what do feelings have to do with anything—especially their pleasure? So if you encounter an emotionally challenged person, you might just be in the presence of an overpleasurer.

7. Financial Problems

Well, I'm sure you can imagine how trouble with finances could easily be characteristic of an overpleasurer. You might be thinking of those poor college students who go a few thousand dollars into debt to buy a great sound system for a very small dorm room in order to satisfy their auditory pleasure.

As the overpleasuring grows, so can the expenses. Yes, we usually picture the guy who overspends to take exotic trips or who buys the bigger, better toy, but women can have this problem, too. I've put in countless hours counseling overpleasurers and their spouses.

This isn't just a matter of money—it's a balance issue. It can involve anyone, from a middle-class overpleasurer who's taking out $200 to do his or her pleasure instead of using it for something that's needed for the family, to the multimillionaire who's squandering vast sums of money.

I know a very wealthy man in the South whose pleasure was risk. He was very prominent in his profession, pulling in millions a year. He bought himself a home computer and quickly got involved with online stock trading. He really became overpleasured with this activity, spending hours studying stocks and trading them on the Internet.

This went on for almost two years. His wife, his successful adult sons, and his accountant all complained as several million dollars trickled away from this otherwise very sane businessman. No, his overpleasuring didn't end up costing him his company, marriage, or family, but there *was* financial strain.

When you're creating debt for pleasure, you may know that it doesn't rate with your plans for retirement or your college funds. Reasonable debt for the reasonable pleasure most of us might experience makes sense, but overpleasurers have a very loose definition of "reasonable." They don't want to have conversations about the percentage of disposable income that's going to their pleasure zones.

I was talking to another successful businessman whose wife's overpleasuring was "helping." She hired housekeepers to help them out around the house. In addition, she hired a nanny for each child and bought a car for the nannies to help *them*—and on and on it went. She was overpleasuring on helping to the tune of more than 60 percent of their disposable income.

The husband figured out that he could retire seven years earlier if only half of this money was going into savings. Again, it didn't break this man, but it was causing undue stress in his marriage.

Financial strain is common with overpleasurers. If you come across it, you can often follow the money trail back to the overpleasurer.

8. Regret

Regret is different for everyone. For some people, it's wishing that they'd been around for their children's sporting events, recitals, and other special moments. For others, it's lamenting the loss of a first or second spouse or missing some other aspect of life.

Regret is often different as we age. I find that most overpleasurers experience their regrets in their 50s and 60s. This is the time when they realize that they've lost out on a relationship with their children or a spouse. They chase down the children who felt unwanted by the overpleasurer—kids who've learned well not to prioritize relationships.

Many of us have families like the one described in the song "Cat's in the Cradle" by Harry Chapin, which tells the story of an overpleasurer who abandoned his son, only to have his son abandon *him* in later years. This is often all too real for the overpleasurer.

Regrets over not saving for retirement often hit over-pleasurers again and again. I'm thinking of a friend of mine in her late 50s who's buying a new house that she and her third husband can barely afford. Her regret will be significant in years to come when her retirement funds are insufficient.

Overpleasurers' memories of their selfishness are often revisited during sober moments. Although they smile on the outside, there's a cloud of sadness in their eyes.

Overpleasurers may also feel regret through their bodies or health. Their lack of responsibility as they pursued their pleasure may have taken its toll physically.

I'll never forget Oscar, known as Oz to the outpatient group I was helping while working on my master's degree. Oz had many great stories about this car crash, that nurse, or that fight, but he was now alone, and his body was paying the price for his overpleasuring.

Regardless of how they experience them, most over-pleasurers have regrets of one kind or another. They wish they could have done this or that, and their occasional sighs during quiet moments are often heard only by them.

These sighs need not exist if we balance our pleasure, relationships, and responsibilities.

9. Rationalization

In addition to all the other symptoms, there's one more gift that an overpleasurer needs: the ability to rationalize.

Imagine a person who's chased the pleasure of amateur car racing, clocking in thousands and thousands of hours working on the vehicle in his garage. He spends weekends traveling with his buddies, and his wife and family support him through weeks of hospital stays and rehabilitation. There's also the lack of college funds or cars for the children, and a decent house or retirement savings for his long-suffering spouse.

Somehow such overpleasurers can rationalize the time commitment, diverted resources, and consequences to themselves and others, including their loved ones. As they age, these rationalizations become irrefutable, unquestionable beliefs.

I know one woman whose pleasure was creativity in the form of painting, but her art career had cost her family a mom. Although she occasionally sold a painting, her absence while she was in the studio, the weekends at art shows, and the shameful things she occasionally did with other artists or those who overappreciated her work all had to be magically rationalized. Even the loss of her first two husbands, who were deemed not understanding, unsupportive, and selfish, and the suggestions of these men's children that she balance art with real life were all rationalized.

In my office in Colorado Springs, I've heard some of the most amazing rationalizations you could imagine; and they aren't specific to age, gender, religious preference, or financial status. Rationalization is by far one of the most painful characteristics of overpleasurers, since it's often what keeps them from seeing most of the earlier symptoms I mentioned. It helps them create a reality in which their irresponsibility and selfishness can make enough sense that they're still able to continue to like themselves day after day. Often they tell those around them to "get over it," "grow up," or "forgive already and move on."

Sad to say, if rationalization crystallizes into a false sense of reality, there's little professionals can do to help. The crying, yelling, or isolation from family members has little impact.

Addictions

Now I want to have a quick but serious discussion of addictions. Overpleasurers are out of balance and gain perspective with some work, education, and self-honesty. Addictions, however, are a totally different ball game.

I work with addicts on a day-to-day basis, and they're a step past the overpleasurer. Most have issues with abandonment; physical, emotional, or sexual abuse; or neglect. They also have limited spiritual, emotional, and moral development, since it was arrested at the onset of the addiction.

It often takes more than education to recover from addictions. Frequently the addict will need to attend some form of 12-step program or therapy group. Counseling is often helpful—I'd strongly recommend seeing a therapist or calling my office to do a telephone therapy session to assess if there's an addiction present and start a treatment plan.

Addiction Characteristics

— **It takes more.** Often addicts no longer receive the same pleasure that they used to from something they formerly enjoyed. Be it golf, alcohol, spending, or food, it takes greater amounts of the substance or activity to get the same buzz. It now requires much more than a little bit for them to feel like they're getting anything out of it.

— **Broken promises.** Frequently addicts have promised themselves and others that they'll stop, but they don't. They start sneaking the substance or activity back into their life. They have cycles of promising, sneaking, and getting caught . . . promising, sneaking, and getting caught. Lying about the activity or substance is a real clue that someone is moving toward an addiction.

— **Consequences.** Addicts often suffer real consequences for their behavior. They might experience severe legal, relationship, financial, or career repercussions directly related to the activity or substance. The addiction takes more of their time and soul, and other areas of life get less and less, eventually leading to significant consequences. Unfortunately, this doesn't necessarily stop addicts from pursuing the activity or substance.

— **Withdrawal.** If addicts stop the substance or the activity, they go through a form of withdrawal. When we think of withdrawal, we imagine the heroin addict screaming and in pain. However, I know many sex addicts who experienced mood swings, headaches, disorientation, and

63

irritability in the first 30 days of not viewing pornography, seeing prostitutes, or gratifying themselves sexually. Try to detox a serious binge addict and you'll see signs of anxiety as well. The form of withdrawal may be different according to the substance, activity, or individual, but it does occur when someone tries to give up an addiction.

— **Denial.** Addicts are often in absolute denial that their activity or substance is a problem for them. You could lay out a case like Perry Mason that the addiction exists and is impacting their life, and their response is still "You're crazy." Denial is a typical earmark of someone with an addiction to any type of activity or substance.

— **Losing control.** Addicts often don't plan to spend as much time or money on the addiction as they do. They have a repeated cycle of losing control when it comes to the activity or substance to which they're addicted.

They intend to do only a little (or "just one") or stay for just a short while, but they don't. They do more or stay longer time and time again, and they can become undependable or unpredictable when partaking in the activity or substance.

❦

The preceding list contains a few of the symptoms of a real addiction. If you feel strongly that you or someone you know is addicted, follow these steps:

1. Get more information about the addiction (consult the Internet or books).

2. Talk to a professional.

3. Locate treatment options.

4. Seek a support group.

5. Confront the addict (stage a professional intervention).

6. Set boundaries and follow through with them.

Being an addict is no fun, and loving someone with an addiction can be extremely difficult. However, seeing that person recover from it is one of life's miracles.

As you seek out pleasure, you must be aware of the dangers of overpleasuring or addiction. They don't lead to a life of balanced pleasure for yourself, nor do they allow you to be responsible and have great relationships.

You deserve maximum pleasure, so continue reading so that you and those you love can experience the greatest (balanced) pleasure possible.

❦ ❦ ❦

Chapter Six

The Underpleasurer

Kelly was an attractive 34-year-old woman who was married to John, a lawyer in the district attorney's office. Kelly was extremely busy, since she worked a corporate job managing almost half of the accounts for a $45 million company.

Kelly had two children in a private school—one in second grade and the other in fourth. She was always on the go and used car time to return calls to her accounts. She was usually rushed picking up the kids, and sometimes they would have to be walked over to the extended-day class a couple times a week due to Kelly's schedule.

In the evening, Kelly had to help her kids with homework and make dinner before John came home. She was a recovering alcoholic, so she went to a few meetings a week when it worked with John's schedule. She also sponsored six women, whom she met with on a fairly regular basis.

Kelly's primary pleasure zone was running. She'd received awards in high school and a scholarship to college for distance running. When you talked to her about this subject, her face lit up. The problem was that Kelly was now an extreme underpleasurer. She was highly responsible and pretty good at keeping up with her primary relationships, but she'd lost her pleasure zone completely.

Kelly, like so many clients who enter my office, was starting to have symptoms of depression and was feeling that life wasn't as much fun as it used to be. She'd been thinking about taking antidepressants before coming in. In other words, Kelly was a classic underpleasurer.

Kurt, another client, was quite a different type of person. He was 43 and really rugged looking. He'd been divorced for six years and worked as an auto mechanic. However, he wasn't just your ordinary mechanic—he was truly gifted at it. He could listen to cars "talk" to get to the bottom of the problem, and he was extremely honest and didn't overcharge. As you might imagine, guys like him are rare, and hence, he was very busy. After he divorced and opened his own company, he found that he had very little time left in his day for anything else.

He would go to work at 5 A.M., and he didn't stop until late at night. He also tried to make time for his children and their special events when he could. He rapidly became an underpleasurer.

Kurt's primary pleasure zone was painting. He had some beautiful artwork from his past before the divorce. Since then, he'd stopped creating. Before he started up his business, he would regularly go out to his patio with a view of the mountains and paint. He used to travel around and sell his paintings at fairs and local shows.

Kurt was quite down about his life. However, after hiring two other mechanics at the shop, he found that he was able to get Wednesdays off until 4 P.M. He used every other Wednesday to start painting again. In six months of reactivating his primary pleasure, he was his old self again, with the big smile he flashed like a jeweled watch.

Underpleasurers are probably much more prevalent than overpleasurers. I've seen countless people who fall into this category. They seem to have a similar set of themes, which I want to outline for two reasons: (1) They can help you if you're currently an underpleasurer; and (2) you'll be much more likely to spot underpleasurers in your life—you know, those friends, family members, co-workers, or neighbors who just seem not to be having any fun.

The Last Time

"So, Harry, when was the last time you had a really good time?" After this question, there's always a long pause. Harry, an underpleasurer, looks at you and then past you as his eyes slowly search for the data.

Harry might come up with: "Well, my cousins and nephew had a birthday party a few months ago." It's true—one of the themes of underpleasurers that I've consistently seen is that they rarely can remember the last time they personally had a really good time.

I know it sounds funny, but ask this question at a party (which underpleasurers probably aren't attending) and see what type of answers you get. I love talking about pleasure and hearing what other people's responses are.

An Entire Year

Along with not remembering the last time they had a really good time is another theme: Rarely are under-pleasurers able to recall an entire year when they were consistently receiving pleasure.

Sadly, some underpleasurers have to go back to when others (such as their parents) were managing their life to remember having consistent pleasure. I know it sounds bizarre that someone would find it so difficult to recollect pleasure. So take a moment and ask yourself when *you* last experienced a primary pleasure for an entire year.

If you want to go further into the pleasure habits of the underpleasuring, ask them who planned their pleasure. You know who set it up: Often the underpleasurer will reference a friend, crazy family member, or someone else as being responsible for their good times.

I myself remember one year that was terrific. My wife, Lisa, and I had a couple of friends who were both psychologists. (As a side note, rarely are people in this profession the best examples of a pleasure lifestyle.) They had a house, a boat, and a Jet Ski on a lake an hour or two from town. I remember going water-skiing and jet skiing regularly, and that was a great year of pleasuring.

I've matured since then and now have my own toys—four-wheelers. You get that warm wind in your hair and experience that outdoorsy feeling. . . . I didn't want you to think that your friend and author was an underpleasurer!

Pleasure Is a Low Priority

One of the themes of underpleasurers is that pleasure in general is a last priority. They rarely even think about it. If you were to look at their day planner or Palm Pilot, you'd readily come to the conclusion that pleasure is a low priority—or no priority.

I sometimes check the calendars of the therapists in my own office to see how they're doing with pleasure. I was shocked just a few weeks ago when I discovered that they were working from 7 A.M. until 6 or 7 P.M.

That schedule might sound reasonable, except that there was something missing: They weren't taking lunches. Well, how can you be helpful to clients if you don't eat, hear the sound of silence or music, or get out of the chair and move around? So after some discussion, everyone agreed that a lunch hour is important, and that we as therapists have value and should also experience a little pleasure in our workday. Since that time, I'm glad to see that the therapists are now getting together for lunch and just chatting. It's a much more fun place to work when the people around you are prioritizing pleasure in their day.

I'm Too Busy

Almost every underpleasurer has this theme: "I'm too busy . . . I don't have time for _____." I can't tell you the number of hours I've spent both professionally and personally listening to the theme of "I'm too busy."

Honestly, I don't get it. I have a full-time practice; and last year I presented at more than 40 conferences, almost all of which were out of town or out of the country. In addition, I wrote three or four books during that period. I get off at 3 P.M. to pick up my kids and take them to music, dance, tae kwon do, or help them with their homework. I'm also active in my spiritual community, and I "date" my wife and make sure that we're individually responsible with our primary pleasure zones. So when people say that they're too busy, and they work 8 to 5 and have no real hobbies—and especially if they don't have children at home—I'm absolutely flabbergasted.

I can only come to a few conclusions:

1. They're real pleasure avoiders.

2. They're happily married and are exhausting each other.

3. They watch so much television that pleasure is being sucked right out of them.

"I'm too busy" is a theme and a state of mind. It reminds me of something that goes on in my house. I live in a neighborhood with lots of children, and it's not uncommon for someone in the group to say, "I'm bored."

Now in our family, we have a saying when people complain "I'm bored" as if they're victims of the universe. We say, "It sounds like you've run out of creativity." I think that the same is true if someone is "too busy" as well. It could be said that with a little creativity, time can be found to create pleasure. With some consistent practice, underpleasurers can actually have fun.

Others Have Greater Value

Another theme that's often prevalent among under-pleasurers is the idea that other people have greater value than they do. They believe that others' needs, issues, desires, and problems are more important than their own personhood. Some even interpret this "less than" view of themselves as a positive quality. My clients of faith spiritualize this undervaluing of themselves.

I have to remind them that they should love others as they do themselves. Now if they did that, most under-pleasurers would be put in jail. Could you honestly imagine somebody telling another person, "No, you can't do that. You have to work and take care of everyone from 6 A.M. till you go to sleep, and don't you dare have pleasure. That's not important—there's no time."

Some of you are laughing. However, not only would this be absurd, it would also be cruel. Trapping someone in a body, soul, and spirit designed for incredible pleasure and then telling that body, soul, and spirit "no" isn't kind on any level.

Yet underpleasurers do this to themselves regularly. Other people have value—*real* value—but it's only equal to our own. We are to treat them as having the same status we do. However, it's true that sometimes their needs are more critical, so there are definitely occasions to put ourselves second to those around us.

As I pen this page, I'm on a plane with my two children, who are to the right of me in seats 25F and 25E. It's the only trip just the three of us have ever taken. You see, my wife went ahead of us to see her mother (Virginia Schaffer), who was in the hospital and has since passed away. She had a stroke while praying at her regular early-morning time—4 A.M. Obviously the needs of my wife, her family, and my children come before any pleasure that I might have planned for this spring-break weekend. Honestly, in this situation, it's a pleasure to commemorate such a great lady by being present for her funeral.

Everyone understands these extreme cases, yet these aren't the only situations where underpleasurers give of themselves. Almost anything can allow them to abandon themselves and lower the priority of their pleasure.

For the underpleasurer, practically any reason to bypass pleasure is acceptable. "Others" are a great excuse to avoid it. Yes, they *are* important, and at times *more* important, but pleasure is also necessary for a healthy life.

It's a Waste of Time

A theme I hear people utilize to rationalize their underpleasuring lifestyle is that "it's a waste of time." I have an analogy for these underpleasurers that I'd like to share here.

I ask them if they own a car. Most of my clients are financially secure, so they say in an almost offended tone, "Of course I do." I suggest that for the next 50,000 miles they do absolutely no oil changes—I want the oil to get nice and thick. Then the friction will increase under the hood, and eventually if we're lucky enough, it can totally lock up the engine, requiring that they get an entirely new engine or car, depending on the price of each.

They look at me as though I'm the nuttiest guy they've ever spoken to. "Are you crazy?" they ask.

I calmly say, "No . . . why?"

"Well, everybody knows that you change the oil every 3,000 miles. Why should I spend thousands to replace an engine when I could spend $20 to change the oil?"

I laugh loudly enough to make them think about the point I'm making. I then ask, "Let me see if I get this straight: You accept the responsibility of maintaining your car, but you balk at the responsibility of maintaining yourself? You see, pleasure is the oil of your life's engine."

If you don't experience pleasure on a regular basis, you create all kinds of "clogging" symptoms in your life. If you're not careful, after years and years of not pleasuring your spirit, soul, or body, your engine might lock up. Most of my clients have that "Aha" look on their face, and then we can move away from the "waste of time" theme.

Maintenance is critical to anything's longevity. This is especially true of human beings. I'm like a mechanic who keeps seeing locked-up engines, so I think that maintenance is the best idea.

I'll never forget Bill, who was a 28-year-old married man with two very small children. I vividly remember him because of where we met. I was in college, and the state hospital called wanting to know if someone would visit a client there. I volunteered for this visit to the hospital, which was less than a mile walk from my college. I went up to the desk and asked the older nurse on duty for Bill.

I met Bill, and we shook hands and walked to a plain room with large windows and older furniture. He was a lanky, tall man who hadn't shaved in a few days and had very sad eyes. We sat down, and he began to tell me about his situation.

Bill was in the hospital because he was suicidal. He obviously was really depressed. I asked him about his outside life. Six months ago, he started an office sales job that was about a 30-mile commute one-way. Around the same time, his wife started some evening college classes so that she could become a nurse. I was curious, so I asked Bill what he did before he started his office job. He said that he was a framer and had built houses for the previous seven years. He'd also run several days a week for about six to eight miles at a time.

I was amazed by how much energy Bill must have had to do hard labor for eight to ten hours a day for years and then run. I asked when he'd scheduled this activity, and he said that he did it at night before his wife started school and after the kids went to bed.

Bill was definitely a physical-pleasure kind of guy. At my young age, I didn't have all this pleasure language to help him, but we did continue to talk. I told him that I thought he was depressed because he'd stopped using his body as much—it was so accustomed to intense lifting, working, and running; and then he just shut it all off and became depressed.

He thought that this was helpful. When I later returned to the state hospital, Bill was no longer there. I have a hunch, though, that he went back to his primary pleasure.

I Was Made for Work

Another person sticks out in my mind as a huge underpleasurer. Bob was a Southern Baptist pastor in Texas. He was a big, six-foot-tall man with an extra 70 or so pounds spread around his large frame. He was loud and fun but very burned-out.

Bob pastored a church of 650 on Sunday. He lived in a little community, so he was a big fish in a small town. Everybody from the mayor, police chief, and high-school principal to the crossing guard at the elementary school knew Bob.

Pastor Bob was hugely overworked. He did almost everything at the church, including cleaning it up and helping with ordering supplies. His wife was the part-time secretary, but keeping up with her five boys was her real job.

Bob taught Sunday school and preached on Sunday morning and evening, as well as on Wednesday night. In addition, he had a 5:30 A.M. prayer meeting on Tuesday with his "Real Men's Group." He also organized many of the youth and senior-citizen activities. Between all this and hospital visits to the sick, helping the local shelter, and attending school-board meetings, Pastor Bob was pushing himself too hard. Although he loved his congregation, he wasn't receiving pleasure.

When I asked him about days off and the hours he worked, he gave me a quick, short answer: "Boy, I was made for work."

"Really?" I asked Pastor Bob. "So if you were made for work, why all the nerves? If you were made for work, why do you have millions of taste buds, colors you can perceive, and things you can feel and hear? Explain to me why you can give and receive so much pleasure if you were just made for work."

"What's your point?" he asked.

"Pastor," I replied, "you were made for pleasure *and* work, not just work. Work is good, but you say that you have a good God. Why wouldn't He want you to also enjoy yourself?"

Pastor Bob finally agreed that he was underpleasuring. After some discussion, we concluded that he really was a calm pleasurer. He grew up in Alabama, and his dad had taken him fishing regularly early in the morning. They would spend hours on their little boat with no noise but that of the jumping fish.

Pastor Bob immediately assigned Fridays as fishing days. Within three months, not only was he symptom free, but he also said that his preaching had never been better.

Many people are like Pastor Bob and have this theme of "all work and no play" in their hearts and lives. However, it's a sure formula for a life that's extremely out of balance. For these people, it's not always about making more money (I'm convinced that this wasn't Pastor Bob's motive); it's just that they feel guilty if they're not being productive. I used to be much like this with my full-time work and school.

I learned the secret, though . . . it's the power of pleasure. When I experience this regularly, my creative juices keep flowing, my productivity goes way up and stays there consistently, and I have a much better attitude about life. My friends, co-workers, and family would probably say that my pleasuring is very much worth it.

That's Selfish

"That's selfish" is the last theme in our discussion. This is a regular comment by underpleasurers about the behavior of both the overpleasurer and the balanced pleasurer. Now they may have a point about the overpleasurer, but even the balanced pleasurer—who makes time for meditation, volleyball, making pottery, and hiking—is viewed as selfish.

Now I'm sorry, but I'm going to have to be clinical for just a little bit here. I want to say something very simple but very valuable, especially to underpleasurers: "Self exists." That's right—I told you it was simple. We each have a self that's separate from all the other "selves" out there.

Now that we know we have a self, we need to evaluate how we're managing it. Remember our discussion about cars? You can drive down a street in any city and see a car that's well cared for, no matter how old it is. It's washed, waxed, and vacuumed regularly. It gets tune-ups and oil changes, and its air filters are replaced periodically. The really, really cared-for vehicle gets the occasional detailing and even a special air freshener for a new-car smell.

Then on the same street in the city, there's the uncared-for car—you know, the one where the tires are barely legal because the tread is so worn, a hubcap is missing on a back wheel, and the dashboard has a crack or two. In such a car, you can't tell what part is dirt and what part is the result of a science project that went really bad.

You see, the owners of these two cars have very different values when it comes to their property. For one, the car exists and therefore there's maintenance to do. For the other owner, the car scarcely registers as an object and really has no value to be maintained. When the guy who doesn't take care of his car sees the other owner responsibly washing and waxing *his*, he just thinks that guy might be a loser or at least that he's overvaluing his car.

Underpleasurers rarely see the responsibility of self and the need to be delighted. Self exists, and to utilize the power of pleasure is simply to take responsibility for the tremendous individual you are.

You're an amazing being in your soul, spirit, and body. If you regularly find pleasure for yourself, that's not selfish—it's responsible. I know that the power of pleasure allows me the opportunity to increase my joy of living and productivity, decrease my stress level, and touch more people's lives positively.

So when I take a "Doug day" or a "Doug afternoon" for pleasuring, I know that I'm actually helping others in the long term. I'm less burned-out and more pleasant, and I actually enjoy my clients as individuals as they share both their hurts and their goals for improvement.

Balanced pleasuring isn't actually selfish in the long run . . . it's just being responsible with the "car" I was given. So if you're an underpleasurer, just look at the vehicle you're driving. If it needs some tender loving care, go ahead and keep reading. Likewise, if you know some underpleasurers who are driving by you in the lanes of life, encourage them to seek out the power of delight that you've discovered on *your* drive.

The Deprivation Cycle

I want to illustrate a cycle of deprivation that I see very regularly, especially in underpleasurers. Recognition of this cycle can help them see the red flags along the way so that they can make a U-turn toward pleasuring.

1. Irresponsibility

Now nobody wants to be irresponsible, especially not underpleasurers. Generally speaking, they aren't just responsible . . . they're *super*-responsible. They take care with relationships and other things but not with their own pleasuring.

Yet this is the first step in the cycle of pleasure deprivation. Underpleasurers don't make a proactive plan for their enjoyment. Again, you just have to look at their day planner to see evidence of this.

So without a plan for pleasure, they only receive pleasures accidentally, not intentionally. If they do make a plan, it can easily be changed for many reasons. This irresponsibility in terms of pleasure planning is the first step in the cycle of deprivation.

2. Rationalizations

As a counselor, I know that when someone isn't responsible in an area of their life, they often have rationalizations. Take, for instance, people who struggle with food, time, or money. Many reasons or rationalizations follow to explain why they can't say no to chocolate, don't exercise, don't go to bed on time, or don't get paid enough.

So it is with underpleasurers. Many of the themes we discussed can be their mantra of rationalization. They might say, "I have no need [or time or money] to . . ." or "That sounds silly [or risky]."

It's actually a stage of deprivation that you can identify. Unlike with irresponsibility, it can take years to really recognize that someone is rationalizing their lack of pleasuring. I know couples who've been married for well over a decade before they realized that one spouse was really an underpleasurer.

When you hear a rationalization, you know to take note, but don't assume that someone is an underpleasurer just because he or she comes up with a legitimate reason not to indulge in pleasure. If, however, you see a pattern of such rationalizations, then you're probably in the presence of an underpleasurer.

3. Deprivation

Here it is: the result of underpleasurers' not planning for pleasure—deprivation. It isn't a place that they plan to arrive at, but they get there nonetheless.

You'll travel a long road to get to deprivation, and then you'll realize there's a conflict between you and where you're going. The best analogy I can give you is a Colorado one.

In plain view of everyone who lives in Colorado Springs is Pikes Peak—an ominous 14,000-foot mountain. The faint of heart who like their bodies take the wonderful cog railway to reach the top.

And then there's the walking trail. It starts off like many trails in Colorado: beautiful and very doable. Then it begins to climb and climb. Herein lies the problem—

as you ascend, it takes more energy for your body to move, it gets colder, and there's considerably less oxygen to supply the basic fuel for the climb.

At some point, you're stopping more than you're walking. You can hear yourself breathe and feel the state of deprivation that you're in. It's not fun at all—you look the same, but your body is fighting you as you keep climbing.

This is what happens to underpleasurers. They arrive at a deprivation point. It's harder for them to deal with life, responsibilities, or much of anything. They feel jammed, and often the underpleasurers themselves aren't the only ones who pay for it.

In deprivation, you can't seem to function as you want or should. You feel the disparity between what life is requiring of you and what's inside of you. It's as if you're reaching into the cupboard of your heart, body, and spirit, only to find that it's empty. You think, *Now what?* And a worse thing happens: You don't know what to do.

Deprivation can be avoided as you learn to harness the power of pleasure, yet if it isn't dealt with, more stages will follow.

4. Anger

The next step after deprivation is anger. You might be thinking, *Oh yeah, underpleasurers are probably angry at themselves as they look in the mirror.* This would be reasonable thought—the anger should be aimed at the perpetrator, right? Yes, that would be rational, but remember that at this point we're not necessarily dealing with rational individuals . . . we're talking about people in a state of deprivation.

Like the mountain climbers, they're in pain, have difficulty breathing, and wonder why they're there; as well as being confused, desperate, dehydrated, and often hungry. These people aren't rational (believe me, I know—I've seen my share); they're hurting and angry. So whom do they get mad at?

That's right, they blame those closest to them and the people who are more responsible: "You made me do this . . . this is insane . . . you won't wait up . . . *you* still have water and food . . . you're being selfish . . . you knew this would happen."

Scenes such as this can get really ugly. That's why you either climb with really good friends or with strangers; otherwise, when deprivation hits, it can damage a weaker relationship.

Much like climbers, underpleasurers who hit deprivation and move to anger aim it at those closest to them. First it's their spouse: "You don't help enough [or do enough or provide enough]. You're going out [or playing, laughing, or having some other kind of fun]—how could you?"

Then the anger trickles out all over the place, sometimes back to the family of origin: "My parents or siblings are never there for me when I need them. They have other plans and can't ever help me." Then underpleasurers turn to their children: "Don't I do enough for you? Get it yourself—you're lazy" or "Shut up, and don't ask me again. What were you thinking?"

Friends, neighbors, and co-workers don't get off scot-free either. They get their fair share of gossip, backbiting, or other passive-aggressive games. If you're taking care of yourself, often your responsibility will make underpleasurers even angrier.

I'll never forget one co-worker I had in a psychiatric hospital. This woman was a laundry list of bad choices and underpleasuring. "Fun" was the last adjective you would use to describe her. You can imagine her anger when a few of us students would have a crack-up time while doing our duties. If you've worked in a larger environment, you've most likely been face-to-face or cubicle-to-cubicle with an underpleasurer who's in the anger stage.

With people such as this, you can invite them to pleasure, but few will come. I recommend that you don't joke around with them or go into detail about your pleasures that took place over the weekend—you'll just put them over the edge (and that wouldn't be nice).

5. Symptom Cluster

As an underpleasurer continues in pleasure deprivation, a symptom cluster will evolve. Although it's unique to the individual, there are some basic things to look for.

First is a behavior that seems to preoccupy them but doesn't give them pleasure. This is tricky, though, because a balanced pleasurer or overpleasurer could be engaging in exactly the same activity (such as crocheting for hours), yet for the underpleasurer, there's no real pleasure associated with it. If, for example, balanced pleasurers with touch and creativity pleasure zones were to crochet for two hours, they'd feel energized and ready for reentry into life.

However, an underpleasurer doesn't report deriving any enjoyment from the preoccupying behavior. What my underpleasuring clients describe is that it's just like checking off another box. They don't feel charged in a positive way. They could crochet, clean out their kitchen drawers, or scrub toilets, and all would be rated the same on the pleasure scale.

The most common preoccupying behavior of underpleasurers is watching television. They can do this for hours a day for years and decades. They remember very little of what they watch and are drained afterward. A balanced pleasurer or overpleasurer whose pleasure zone is entertainment is different: They want to talk about it with someone—the characters, plot, or humor is delightful to them. Hopefully you can see the difference.

The second feature is that their preoccupying behavior takes up significant amounts of time. In most cases, underpleasurers have 4 to 20 hours of preoccupation per week.

A third thing to look for is a preoccupation of thought. Underpleasurers tend to spend way too much time thinking about one thing. For some, it's their bad childhood: sexual, physical, or emotional abuse. For others, it's how bad their current life or relationships are. For still others, it can be politics, religion, or school-board or other community-agency issues.

Again, these focused thoughts can absorb hours in the course of a day or week, but they still don't bring pleasure. Think of the grandmother who worries constantly about her kids, grandkids, and neighbors but who doesn't receive enjoyment from all of her thoughts.

Defensiveness is also part of the symptom cluster of underpleasurers, who often have an invisible sign around them that says, "Do not disturb" or "Enter at your own risk." Underpleasurers aren't having fun and question anybody who is. The answer they give to people who ask them what's going on is usually defensiveness in the form of silence, switching the subject, or just a glare of *Can't you read my sign? It says, "Do not disturb."*

6. Repeat or Responsibility

Here's the final part of the cycle of deprivation: repeat or responsibility. Almost all of us have played the game of *Monopoly* as children or adults: You roll the dice and go around the board. When you pass "GO," you get to collect your $200 and begin to move around it again. To underpleasurers who start taking responsibility for pleasure, it's as if they get another chance to go around the board.

This time, they get to utilize the power of pleasure. They're able to see the different colors on the board of life. They want to take that stroll down St. James Place or the Boardwalk. They put it on the calendar and begin to reverse the cycle of deprivation. They have less anger, fewer rationalizations, and more energy to climb the "Pikes Peak" of their life. They're not blaming others and actually begin to like those who are also enjoying life.

Underpleasurers who don't take responsibility condemn themselves to repeat the same cycle and confront all of the individuals they love with their deprivation, anger, and rationalizations. It's so odd, but they often don't see how their lack of pleasuring really passes the same sentence on everyone around them. Often they want to be applauded for their suffering and sacrifice, but over the years they're left alone and feel underappreciated as they stay in "jail," instead of getting out and going around the board of life.

♈

I know that this discussion has many facets. Underpleasuring is probably one of the most common issues people face, but often it goes under the radar and is undetected by others or ourselves. We frequently don't recognize it until we start seeing some of the traits in the cycle of deprivation.

The power of pleasure is so incredible in our lives, yet we often take it for granted, just like light or air. However, we definitely know when we're not getting enough by the way we act and feel.

I remember consulting for a psychiatric hospital that specialized in eating disorders. This was a great facility for people with such diseases. I found myself amazed by the two extremes in this hospital: At the same table, you'd have a very overweight patient sitting next to an anorexic woman who was balding and so skinny that you could almost make out her skull.

As I worked alongside one of the clinicians, I noticed a stark difference between the overeaters (overpleasurers) and the anorexics (underpleasurers). I found that it was much easier to get an overpleasurer to cut back and make changes. It's as if the overpleasurers were stuck on the "yes" button of life and just needed to learn to say no to themselves in some way.

The anorexics (that is, the underpleasurers), in contrast, appeared to be stuck on "no," trying to use the "yes" button. However, it seemed more challenging for them to say yes to themselves than it was for the overeaters to say no.

This is important: If you're an underpleasurer, you may feel as if it's a harder road to travel. It *does* feel that way, but consider what happened to the patients with anorexia: When they could use their will to say yes, their life, health, and physical appearance changed for the better.

You absolutely deserve pleasure. You have a right to feel its power in your life and to experience the pleasures that you were designed for on a regular basis. You have the same worth as everybody else on the planet. Your time to live is limited, so choose the "yes" button to pleasure . . . you'll never regret it!

🌷 🌷 🌷

Chapter Seven

The Balanced Pleasurer

Justin is a 46-year-old commercial real-estate broker and developer. He's constantly starting and closing deals and planning developments—and he's a balanced pleasurer. Justin works really hard when he's on the job. Let me go over his weekly routine.

He exercises at 5 A.M. either by running, going to the gym, or bicycling. He and his wife, Cheri, go on regular dates almost weekly. Tuesday is Dad's night with their three children, and it always has been. After homework on Tuesday, Mom is kicked out of the house to get a break. This schedule is a lot of fun for everyone.

Justin is connected to his spiritual community and has a group of men he meets with on Friday mornings. He fits in his other male friends mostly at lunches here and there, but averages this a few times a month. One of Justin's pleasure zones is touch. Every other Thursday, Micah, his massage therapist, shows up at his downtown office. Justin's secretary, Gina, is very careful to make this happen in his schedule. Her philosophy is "A relaxed boss is a happy boss."

Justin's other pleasure zone is food. He particularly likes unusual sauces. Before Cheri and Justin had children, they both took cooking classes to learn how to make them. They're experts at creating sauces for almost any dish. Justin also has a pleasure zone of prayer and meditation. He takes what he calls a "sacred break" during each day to read spiritual literature, clear his mind, and be still. He says that it doesn't take long to achieve this if you're consistent about it.

Justin is a very busy guy, like so many of us, yet he balances life with pleasure. He and Cheri get a night away every once in a while. They also take family hikes, weekend lake trips, and at least one five-day vacation a year to various locations.

Candy lives a totally different lifestyle from Justin's. She's the mother of two elementary-school-aged children, and she also is a full-time RN. She really feels pressured to keep life balanced, but she too is a balanced pleasurer. She made arrangements with her hospital and her husband, Art, to go to work at 6 A.M. and leave by 2 P.M. The school is close enough to the hospital that she gets to walk for about 45 minutes right before the children get out. (Of course, living in California, she's not the only power walker picking up kids.)

Candy and Art also schedule a Mom's night out (yes, I recommend this to all married couples with children). She occasionally sees a movie with girlfriends, but mostly her pleasure zone is calm. She soaks in a Jacuzzi at the gym, and she'll sit on the beach with a book or just relax in safe areas outdoors. She reports feeling reenergized afterward.

Candy is also a taste-pleasure person with an affinity for chocolate. She limits this to either an occasional small binge or no more than two pieces a day. She'll sneak off to a quiet place in the nurses' lounge to open her very rich piece of chocolate and place it in her mouth. She has a rule: "No chewing allowed." She just lets it melt—the whole process takes about two minutes, but nothing else exists for her during that time.

She dates Art about three times a month. Her sisters are a primary support for her, and she sees them or talks to them on the phone regularly. Three of the four sisters live within 15 minutes of one other.

Candy is a busy woman, but she's also a balanced pleasurer. Both Justin and Candy have maintained balanced pleasuring for years. Life may try to throw things off (and is sometimes successful), but for the most part their commitment to pleasure brings it all back into balance.

The Journey

Being a balanced pleasurer is more a journey than a destination. Life circumstances are only one of the variables in trying to stay balanced. Often the greater enemy of balanced pleasuring is ourselves, not our environment.

Let's go back to Justin. He wasn't always balanced. In earlier years, he was almost a workaholic and an exercise-aholic. He put in very long days several times a week, abandoning Cheri to raise the children with very little support. He worked out daily to the point of obsession. His primary need for physical contact was so inadequately met that the only time he reported being touched was during intimacy with his wife.

I remember meeting Justin when he and Cheri were struggling in their marriage. Justin's lack of balance was really a major factor in weakening their relationship. Justin didn't come on board right away. I remember the conversation we had about having more fun and going on vacations. Justin really thought I was off my rocker. He described his childhood with his parents, who had immigrated to America, started a dry-cleaning business, and put in all kinds of crazy hours. He and his brother and sister had worked since they were very little.

He talked about the family not having a vacation for many years while he was growing up. I stopped him and asked when he'd last taken a vacation with *his* family that didn't involve any business. He looked over at Cheri to rescue him. They finally concluded that it had been well over a few years' span.

This was a turning point for Justin to get on board with balancing his pleasure. After a while, he was able to see the value of parenting, dating his wife, and even going on family vacations. Once we threw in the idea of getting massages twice a month, he thought that I was brilliant.

Justin started to experience pleasure. He also realized that a reprieve from the grind helped him. He was nicer and smarter, and he actually had creative ideas just pop into his head. Now Justin is a very balanced pleasurer, but it took an inner journey to explore his values, including life messages from his parents and his goals for his family.

Candy, on the other hand, had been such an under-pleasurer that she was negatively impacting her health and parenting, and she was losing interest in her marriage as a romantic venture. Candy was the oldest of seven children, so she'd been taking care of kids since she was barely in the first grade. She changed their diapers, fed them, and rocked them to sleep. If she was playing, she always had to keep an eye on her brothers and sisters. If they needed help with homework, Mom and Dad didn't have time, so Candy had that job as well. She was highly responsible.

Her journey was also a quest to reflect on her values. I remember that when she really realized she had a self, she started to cry uncontrollably. In the past, she wasn't allowed to be herself—she had to be a function, not a person.

Her discovery that her value was equal to others' was also a big step. Then she was able to look at how she was abandoning her body to bad food habits and lack of exercise. She could also address the overtime issues at the hospital where she was "needed."

The more difficult part of her journey was seeing how she was abandoning her husband and her own sexuality. He wasn't a person either—just a helper with all the stuff they had to do.

Candy was a classic underpleasurer. She was only able to gain a little insight and structural change at a time. She reported that the day she found the resolve to ask her supervisor if she could come in and leave earlier was like entering the twilight zone. She couldn't even imagine questioning the hospital's authority over her life. She didn't think that her need to get a break between work and parenting merited changing her schedule. She was absolutely flabbergasted when her supervisor smiled and told her that she'd done the same thing for a while when her children were in preschool.

You see, becoming a balanced pleasurer takes time. It also means that you'll probably have to examine some issues along the way. Let's discuss four major issues to look at on the journey of becoming a balanced pleasurer.

1. Family Messages

First, most of us have to look at our family's messages and teachings about pleasure, as well as the example they set. Some of our parents were selfish overpleasurers, whether their pleasure was hunting, bingo, or eating. For example, I was in an airplane one time, and on the monitor there was a preview of a show about parenting. Every time a child did something the parents approved of, they gave him or her a treat, just as you would a dog. The family message about food was all about pleasure.

Looking at our family's messages about over- or underpleasuring is one step in the journey of becoming a balanced pleasurer. The goal isn't about determining right or wrong . . . it's more than that. Rather, it's about establishing a point of origin for some of the feelings and thoughts attached to any out-of-balance behaviors.

2. Values

The journey of becoming a balanced pleasurer probably entails addressing the issue of values. Often adjusting our sense of self-worth to be equal to everyone else's is important in becoming a successful pleasurer. For some of us, it's the journey of seeing others as having value, and raising that value up to our own. More often, it's the journey of our becoming aware of the truth that *our* value is equal to that of the people around us.

Either way, the adjustment is necessary for us to become a balanced pleasurer. It's definitely worth the effort. This may be a difficult part of the journey, but it's clearly worthwhile.

3. Rationalizations

Looking at our rationalizations, lies, or excuses is an important step in becoming a balanced pleasurer. I'm sure you've heard the saying "They said it so much that they believed it was true." Regularly probing our beliefs and questioning their validity and function in our life is definitely an ongoing process. If you're seeking to become a balanced pleasurer, in this stage of the journey you can pause and relinquish old "friends" (that is, beliefs) that aren't working and adopt new ones. This is all a part of the path to becoming a balanced pleasurer.

4. Responsibility

Looking at your responsibility is the last gate to walk through before a true change can occur. This gate often seems wide and high when you first look at it. It appears overwhelmingly massive and heavy. You almost don't want to touch it for fear of what might happen.

On the one hand, your fear is that it might open. You slowly reach toward it, arm outstretched, worrying about what might occur. If the gate opens, you might have to be responsible. Oh, the horror of what that could bring!

On the other hand, as you reach out to push against it, you fear that it won't move or open for you now and that your greatest fear of all might come true: *I'm doomed to stay the same.* The gate of responsibility is large, and everyone who seeks balance must push against it.

This reminds me of a classic scene from *The Pilgrim's Progress,* which I read as a very young man. Christian, the main character, was told that the right path is the "straight and narrow" one. He had undertaken many journeys, but he was now looking at two very large, ferocious lions. Their loud roars were enough to make his blood run cold. Their teeth were something out of a dinosaur movie. Their eyes were the worst: wild, hungry, mean, and unrelentingly piercing.

Christian had to decide: *Do I go back? Do I go off the path, which has not been a wise move in the past? Or do I advance and go against all that my senses tell me and against all that seems right?*

Christian chose to stay on the path, challenging all that he knew, believed, and experienced. He walked slowly toward the giant roaring lions. As he did so, his situation was so frightening that he could barely keep his eyes open. To his utter surprise, though, he noticed that the lions were chained up, something he hadn't been able to see earlier. He stayed close to the center of the path, and the lions roared but couldn't touch him.

That's how it often feels for the person who seeks to be a balanced pleasurer. They feel the pressure of their past beliefs, paradigms, and rationalizations roaring at them, calling them back or pushing them off the path. Then, as they open the gate of responsibility, they find it oddly weightless—it's as if it's made of some super-duper light aluminum. The gate opens wider and wider with ease. They walk past the beliefs that have caused them to be irresponsible in the past and form new beliefs step-by-step.

These new beliefs trigger new behaviors. With repetition, these become a pattern, which in turn ages into a habit, and then ultimately matures into a lifestyle. Like a snake that sheds an old skin, over time and with persistence, a former over- or underpleasurer becomes a balanced pleasurer.

Wow, what a beauty a balanced pleasure is to behold! As we say in Colorado, the view is worth the climb. Such is the journey to becoming a balanced pleasurer. This doesn't happen all at one time, nor do we arrive there permanently. We aim only to stay honest and improve. There's a saying in 12-step groups: "Progress, not perfection."

So as you stay on the path of your goal, keep walking in order to really experience the power of pleasure flowing through your life. Sometimes the way is arduous, but occasionally you just get to enjoy the walk, the wind, and the view.

The Triangle of Balance

So, what are we really talking about when we're discussing balance? The best way to address this is to look at a triangle.

A perfect triangle has three equal angles. This is important because if one angle gets smaller, one or both of the others will also be affected.

That's how it is with balance. It isn't so much about focusing on a single thing to the point that the other equally important aspects of life get out of balance. I heard someone once say that success isn't success if it comes at the cost of another area of your life. This truth is really crucial in becoming a balanced pleasurer.

Let's discuss this triangle one angle at a time. As we investigate each one closely, we can evaluate our state of balance. Afterward, we can also back up and really see what our triangle looks like as a whole.

Angle #1: Relationships

Whether we like it or not, we'll always be in relationships. Everyone wants to be valued, cherished, and considered important by others. We also like to give to others and extend our spirit, soul, and body to them.

Even when our friends or family members ask us to forgo a Saturday morning to help them move, we smile because at least they thought of us first. We all need to have relationships in order to be in balance, and we need a variety of them to stay sane and have a great time in life. Let's review briefly the different types of relationships.

Primary relationships are exactly that—primary. They involve those whom you're connected to by blood or marriage. If you're in a serious romantic relationship, this would definitely qualify. Your mother, father, and siblings are also significant primary relationships, as are your children, if you have them (including stepchildren or kids who are adopted). If you feel a connection to a deity, this would also fall into a primary-relationship category.

Now as a therapist, I know that not all primary relationships are what they should be. I'm aware that abuse, neglect, abandonment, and cruel words are often present. However, when your child or spouse shines at what he or she does, there are few feelings that are greater. Primary relationships, regardless of the state they're currently in, are still primary. These people were, and will remain, the principal shapers and influences in your life.

Secondary relationships also make up a nice portion of your life. These are your long-term, seasonal, or "convenience" friends. They might be neighbors or people in your social circle. They might be friends of your parents or children, or comrades in a social, spiritual, or political cause.

These secondary relationships are your "buds"—the people you like to hang out with . . . those you "do" life with. You know their spouses, their kids, and their flaws. They're the people you tend to love regardless of their shortcomings.

We all like having friends. Take the TV shows *Friends* and *Seinfeld,* for example: Both were about a group of people in a secondary relationship who take on life together. For us older folks, there was *M.A.S.H.,* about a bunch of army peers who are friends. Then who could forget *Happy Days* with The Fonz, Richie, and Howard? I think you get the point. We love to participate in secondary relationships with people who support us, challenge us, and usually forgive us even when we make mistakes.

Life supplies numerous secondary relationships. As you grow, often they change (with a geographical or social move, for instance). As your values shift—say, from being a party animal in college to being a loving parent—so will your relationships.

It's essential to maintain and sustain current secondary relationships and keep the doors open for new ones. This group of people may be even more important to those individuals whose primary relationships are painful, strained, or geographically challenging.

Acquaintance relationships are really fun, too. They're the waiters, cabbies, clerks where you shop, neighbors farther down the street, or some of the people at work or school. These are the outer-fringe people in your life—the ones you smile at because you see each other regularly. Sometimes you know their names, but rarely do you know very much about them.

Relationships are critical to all of us, whether they're primary, secondary, or acquaintance. Keeping them as a priority is one of the angles of the triangle of balance.

As you may recall, both Justin and Candy learned how to make time for their spouses, children, and even their friends. They had to be creative about doing so. Whether it was taking a power walk together or going out to lunch, they maintained social ties as a part of their balanced experience.

One of the things I love about my friends is that they see me differently from the way I see myself. They hear what I say more objectively and can challenge my logic.

I remember when a group of us guys were hanging around a table together. One friend started to talk about a problem he was having with an employee. As he spoke, we all listened, and he asked the hardest question a person ever asks: "What do you think?"

Each man at the table added a different perspective to his problem. As the conversation ended, the original speaker was aware that his need to be liked was a great issue. He was able to resolve this issue because he had friends.

Angle #2: Responsibilities

Now, class, settle down! How many times have we heard these familiar words in elementary, junior high, and high school? Often they were uttered by well-meaning teachers after they hit on a topic that the class wasn't willing to discuss rationally.

I know that "responsibility" isn't a favored subject in Western culture. I've earned four degrees after high school, and there wasn't one course available on this subject.

Often at school or work, there's blame and scapegoating going on with respect to any given problem. The teachers blame the parents, who in turn find fault with the schools, spiritual communities, and police. Employers are amazed by how little their employees know about and accept responsibility.

So my goal here isn't to teach a course; rather, it's just to highlight three major areas of responsibility, which make up the second angle of the balanced triangle. Remember, if there's slack here, it impacts the other angles.

Finances

This is a really big area where we have to act like adults. As we mature, we accept our place in the ranks of adulthood. This status means that we're willing to be financially responsible. Now we all hear about how the number of bankruptcies is going way up. More and more people are having difficulty managing their debt-to-earnings ratio.

When you buy everything you see instead of what you can afford, you get in trouble. The amount of income you earn doesn't matter either. I've known people who make almost a million dollars a year and find themselves living paycheck to paycheck.

Emotional financial living has replaced principled money management in the last 30 to 40 years. So we all must be careful not to be sucked into a "see and spend" lifestyle.

Here's what happens once you start amassing significant debt without balancing savings: You create anxiety, including worries that you can't make the payments. You start paying off the interest only, which cuts into your future earnings.

You want to look normal, so you still shop, go out to eat, and have an extravagant Christmas because you don't want others to know that you're being irresponsible. Thus begins a cycle of secrecy that cripples your judgment.

Now because of this recklessness, there's increased friction in your marriage, which then affects you socially because you don't want to fight around others and have them find out about your marital problems. The anxiety starts moving toward regret, fear, and self-loathing; and you begin to disrespect yourself or your spouse—or both. These attitudes eventually extend to the ever-needy children as you explode at them and say something that you end up being sorry for . . . and the problem continues.

As financial irresponsibility grows, you become much more self-focused (pain does that). The generous side of you shrinks. You become wary of those who ask you for financial help because you honestly can't even support yourself properly.

Fortunately, if you're in your 20s, this is just part of growing up. As you age, however, the shame of this financial irresponsibility grows. As you move into your 50s and 60s, the almost insurmountableness of the problem becomes overwhelming.

In contrast, financial *responsibility* has exactly the opposite impact on us as human beings. People or couples who live below their means can give more to others and also save. As they do so, they're able to make bigger and wiser choices. They like themselves a lot better and are more open to relationships.

They're not secretly ashamed. They can go out with peers as they wish. They feel good about what they can provide for their children and experience moments that are a reward for these investments.

Financially responsible people are generally principle based in how they deal with their money. A sale isn't an enticement toward debt. They see a loan as something to pay off quickly. They tend to sacrifice early in life and "party" later.

I think that you can see how financial responsibility can impact the other parts of the triangle. As you look at these angles, you might acknowledge your immaturity or see areas where you need to grow—this is fine as you take the journey toward having the power of pleasure flow through your life.

The balanced triangle lets us see potential blockages to long-term pleasure. So just pause, look at the issue, and glean what you can.

Health

A second part of the angle of responsibility is our health. We all have a few issues in this area based on our genetic makeup, but some of us fare better than others. I think of my wife, who's had almost perfect health over our 20 years of marriage. A few of us have to work harder to maintain healthy bodies.

However, if we're irresponsible about our physical well-being, we can suffer very significant consequences that affect all of our relationships. We find ourselves impacting the people we love with our own choices.

Health responsibility basically has three prongs to it. The first is to eat no more than the number of calories you would burn in a day (this can vary from day to day if you sit for hours on end in a chair like I do during the workweek). In addition to water (not soda), healthy food for your body needs to be a major part of your dietary intake.

The second prong of health responsibility is exercise. Now I don't mean that you have to work out daily or even intensely—just include some regular exercise weekly (remote-control pushing isn't officially exercise!).

The third prong of health responsibility is sleep. Your body, soul, and spirit need rest. As I'm writing this, I'm in Chicago's O'Hare International Airport. Today there were really bad winds, so all flights have been delayed, and some passengers like myself have also been in this and previous airports for more than ten hours. It's 10:10 P.M. by my watch, and people all around me are getting touchy. They're throwing their suitcases down and talking like sailors—why? Yes, it's true that they're frustrated, but really they're all exhausted.

If we're responsible by eating reasonably and healthfully, exercising, sleeping, and (of course) taking our medications or following our doctors' orders, we can maintain reasonable health. Wellness is critical in the responsibility part of the triangle. Those who neglect it usually use endless time, energy, and financial resources trying to regain what they could have sustained with different ideals and behaviors.

I'm reminded of my stepfather, Bob, when I think about this. In his 30s, Bob was a healthy man. He slept well most of the time, worked hard on a street crew, and ate reasonably for his generation.

He did, however, have a really bad habit: He smoked packs of Marlboro cigarettes daily. He started coughing at night, and this disturbed his sleep, which lowered his immunity. He would get sick more often, and his energy decreased rapidly. While I was in college, he learned that he had cancer. He underwent surgery and had a portion of his throat taken out. He had to use a device to speak—and yes, he still smoked.

Bob and my mother spent much of their time, energy, and money on doctors' visits, hospital stays, lab work, and treatments, yet he died at age 44. He weighed less than 100 pounds at the time and was a shadow of his earlier robust self.

His sickness absorbed any savings that he and my mother had accumulated. She had to stop working for a while to care for him. His death made us all grieve, and we were all saddened by his health irresponsibility, which affected every aspect of his life and impacted everyone who knew him.

On the other hand, people who are reasonably healthy can enjoy life. They have a better attitude and higher self-esteem. I notice this in the summertime. Like all children, mine love to go swimming. The dads and moms who have reasonably fit bodies jump in and get wet and walk around with no shame (yes, some are even proud). Those who aren't responsible about their health avoid the water or the pool altogether.

Healthier people like to play more and do things with their friends, family, and children. Our health responsibility is our own.

I know that just like everybody, I have a responsibility for my health. I have hypothyroidism (please don't e-mail me about all the cures). I follow my doctor's orders and eat right and exercise. I'm not using this as an excuse for gaining extra pounds. I stay reasonable about my weight and diet (I'm not a nut here—I enjoy sweets at regular intervals).

If I didn't take care of my health issues, there would be several repercussions:

- My quality of work (that is, my counseling) would suffer.

- I'd be more negative and probably would be asked to speak less (which would mean a loss of income).

- I'd be less fun with my wife, children, and friends.

- I would definitely shy away from my more fit and energetic peers (I might actually resent them).

- I wouldn't write as much, and probably not at all (forget about penning books at 10 P.M. in airports!).

I choose to be responsible with my health because I need energy for my wife, children, and other family members. I want to attract fit friends and to be like them. I also want to be able to write, since I really get pleasure from sharing ideas that help improve others' lives.

The Future

So far, all of our discussion has been about the present. The third part of this angle of responsibility is the future.

We all have at least some future ahead of us. None of us can know what life will throw at us, but we can prepare for the basic stages we'll go through.

It's wise to look at your life as if it were a movie instead of a series of photographs. In whatever chapter or scene you're in, you need to consider the future ones. If you're in your 20s, prepare through education or by working toward a down payment on your house and investments. Ready yourself for marriage and parenting. In your 30s, start looking seriously at retirement, enjoy your family, and save for your children's college education and cars. In your 40s, enjoy and exploit your gifts and talents, give responsibly, and prepare for your parents' needs as they age. In your 50s, form a plan for retirement that you can live with.

The future is like a locomotive that approaches over time and eventually arrives. Those people who've been irresponsible with the future are hit hardest by life's blows. They have no resources for housing or college funds. Later they have no money to invest for a secure retirement and have nothing to give those they love.

For those who are irresponsible with the future, fear, shame, guilt, and sometimes a brazen arrogance builds up over their lifetime. Rationalizations for poor choices clutter their self-perception, limiting their growth. Their relationships are impacted, but they hardly notice the lack of stable adults in their life except when they need a loan or a cosigner.

Those who prepare for the future have a different aim. They don't believe that they can control what's going to happen, but they plan for the large issues. They save for their wedding, down payments, college funds, and retirement; and they carry medical and life insurance throughout their lives. They even view cars and their children's marriages as something to look forward to and not dread. They don't bow their heads and say "sorry" to their kids at critical times in their development.

Those who prepare for the future don't experience life with so much apprehension, fear, or guilt or with so many rationalizations. They're generally more honest with themselves, and although they can't control the future, they have more optimism, which then permeates their lives, relationships, and pleasures.

✿

I know that for some of you this part of the triangle has been a walk in the park. Others of you might be mad at me for even talking about this subject matter.

During my more than 18 years as a counselor, I've seen how the angle of responsibility and its effect on relationships have a great impact on our pleasure. It's akin to marriage counseling, where the therapist will have to discuss hard issues such as sex, dating, money, and parenting if he or she is going to help the couple.

The goal of these conversations is to help you achieve more pleasure in your life. As you continue to read, you'll see that this will make more sense. Now let's go to the final angle of the triangle of balance.

Angle #3: Pleasure

That's right—the third angle of the triangle of balance is pleasure. You absolutely deserve to discover, maintain, and sustain pleasure in your life. It's just as significant as the other two angles. You're absolutely made for pleasure, just as you're made for relationships and responsibility. Humans crave it in the same way that they do connecting or making good choices.

I know, I can hear the cynic in some of the under-pleasurers, questioning, "So, Dr. Weiss, are you saying that pleasure is vital to life?" Yes, I'm absolutely saying that! I'm aware that there are some places where—due to oppression, tyranny, and economic disasters—there's little pleasure . . . but even there, the *desire* for it exists.

Pleasure is one of the greatest parts of being human. Although our animal friends enjoy the wind, the snow, or even a tasty treat if they can get something off our table, they can't delight in the magnificent art, science, or other pleasures that are distinctly human (again, don't e-mail me about what animals are capable of—I love them, and I will give your e-mails to Moses, my dog, to get pleasure from, if you think that he'd get excited about your comments).

Deriving pleasure from all three angles is probably the least-taught concept. Most of us, whether we listened or not, probably heard some voice telling us how to treat people:

- "Don't lie."

- "Do unto others as you would have them do unto you."

- "What comes around goes around."

- "Be nice, kind, and thoughtful."

In like manner, there were probably voices talking to us about responsibility. We heard:

- "Eat to live—don't live to eat."
- "Work hard and save money."
- "Think about the future."

Growing up, I honestly don't remember any real voices for pleasure other than kids saying, "Hey, let's go have fun." But the kid who had the idea always defined "fun." In our childhood, most of us drew some significant blanks in our development of pleasure. We eventually figured out a few things we wanted in life but weren't really confident how to go about getting them.

That's why the power of pleasure is so important. Before you finish reading these pages, you'll be able to identify your pleasure zones and make plans to activate, maintain, sustain, and re-create enjoyment for yourself for a lifetime.

Integrating the triangle of balance is so valuable. You might be really good at relationships but be bad at finances and pleasure. You could excel at responsibility but have significant weakness in relationships and pleasure. You might get an A+ in pleasure but be less than wonderful at relationships or responsibility (in this case, life is a party, but you don't know who's paying for it!).

Neglecting the triangle of balance can lead to major consequences for the individual, but he or she isn't the only one who's suffering. People who are in relationships with someone whose triangle is out of whack also suffer. Here's another kicker: This imbalance can be taught and last hundreds of years in a family, impacting not only one generation, but many.

An individual with a balanced triangle is a beautiful thing. It's like watching a finely trained athlete or performer or the beauty of an amazing engine or other mechanical structure.

People with a balanced triangle have positive primary, secondary, and acquaintance relationships (as much as anyone can). They're reasonably responsible with their finances, health, and future. They know their pleasure zones and make adequate time for the familiar pleasures and experiment with new ones.

Now there are people who intuitively maintain their triangle of balance. For some, it was taught by their parents. For others, it's just a natural ability, like that of an athlete, musician, or artist—they were just born with it and couldn't really tell you how they got it. Unfortunately, most of us don't have a gift for living a balanced-triangle life; we have to develop a skill for it.

Regardless of whether you have the balanced triangle by innate gift or through skill, when you move toward it, you'll find that you can master the power of pleasure in your life. You can adjust the reins in the areas of relationships, responsibilities, and pleasures. You're intentional in the way you go about your life. You're less prone to accidental success that's only temporary. If you develop a balanced triangle, you can teach it to others—even your own children.

I honestly hope that my great-great-great-grandkids will be living a life of balance in pleasure, relationships, and responsibility. I hope that because of this balance, they'll be a positive influence on their spouses, children, neighbors, friends, and acquaintances and those in their community of faith.

I hope that you're getting this whole concept. We all leave the legacy of our triangle of balance. For some of us, it might be what our children have to work through to get to balance. However, I hope that you're ready to pave the way for the generations after you to really live life fully and harness the power of pleasure.

111

Six Characteristics of Balanced Pleasurers

1. Intentionality

Something that's glaringly apparent about all of the balanced pleasurers I've met or coached is their intentionality. Balanced pleasurers don't leave their lives up to chance, emotions, or the whims of those around them.

They set up structure in order to have a balanced triangle. Once they develop or codevelop a plan, they stay focused on it. If and when "life" happens, they're deliberate about getting back on track. It's like dating your spouse after getting married: If it's left to chance, it will only happen here and there—when the planets align just right.

Lisa and I are intentional daters. Before I started traveling, we went out on Friday or Saturday. Then I began speaking at conferences regularly on those days, so we intentionally moved it to Monday or Wednesday, depending on the babysitter's schedule. When life threw us a curveball and our children were both in drama rehearsals on our date-night options, we scheduled it in on Friday morning after we dropped the kids off at school.

You see, because we're intentional, dating consistently stays a part of our marriage. I really think that Lisa and I like each other more because we both make having fun together a priority.

2. Compassion

The trait of compassion stands out to me as another important quality of the balanced pleasurer. This isn't to say an over- or underpleasurer isn't compassionate—I just see it more often in balanced pleasurers.

More often than not, this may be the case because of their personal journey. Most had to face their own faulty thinking, behaviors, and values; and they accepted their flaws before they could become balanced. They can see people more honestly and accept them without a need to fix them.

A second reason why balanced pleasurers might have more compassion is that they have better self-care. When you act responsibly toward yourself, you have more to give to others. When you're ashamed, anxious, or in pain due to deprivation in your life, you have less to give and don't notice others' needs as frequently. As the old adage goes, "You have to have something before you can give it away."

3. Fluid Thinking

One thing I see very commonly with under- and over-pleasurers is black-and-white thinking. What this means is that their thought process is generally in an "either-or" pattern.

Most under- or overpleasurers think in terms of extremes. Balanced pleasurers are much more fluid. Honestly, sometimes it can even be wearisome as they think of several different ways to accomplish the goals at hand. I know this might seem like a strange characteristic, but it's really true. A balanced thinker can easily fit pleasure, relationships, and responsibility together.

Luke, for example, has a primary physical pleasure of intense workouts. His wife informs him that she has to go to work early to prepare for a big meeting with her boss and he needs to take the kids to school. If Luke were a black-and-white overpleasurer, he'd respond, "No way—that's when I go to the gym and run." If he were an underpleasurer, he'd say, "I guess I'll miss working out again. It's not a problem, honey."

Luke isn't either of these types of people . . . he's a fluid thinker. He quickly goes into "both-and" mode. He inquires about when she's leaving—she tells him that it will be 7 A.M. He knows that this is the time when the kids wake up to start their morning.

He gets up at 4:45 A.M. to hit the gym early. He hustles through his workout and returns home by 6 to run for 20 minutes. He quickly showers, and then he tells the kids that he'll stop by McDonald's for their breakfast if they can get ready early enough. He swings by the drive-through and stops at the bank to drop off a deposit. He gets the kids off to school and meets with a mentor-type friend for his own breakfast at work by 9:15.

Luke didn't forget pleasure or compromise his responsibility or relationships for even one minute. He was able to be flexible and adapt. With his "both-and" thinking, he accomplished it all, and his wife was able to leave early as well.

4. Primary Relationships

In my experience, balanced pleasurers usually have pretty good primary relationships. While it's true that it takes two to make a great marriage, the presence of at least one balanced pleasurer helps.

Unlike overpleasurers, who cycle through deprivation, balanced pleasurers don't typically add undue stress to their lives in order to have pleasure. They tend to stay more even-keeled.

Balanced pleasurers usually like to have fun, so dating as well as vacations are part of their lives. The fact that one person in a relationship is balancing pleasure often moves the marriage and the family toward balance, regardless of what the other spouse is doing. Couples who are having fun tend to do better. Also, the general optimism of the balanced pleasurer usually benefits the marriage and family.

5. Positive Secondary Relationships

Balanced pleasurers usually have friends, and they don't normally isolate themselves. They generally value others, so people tend to appreciate them as well.

Taking initiative isn't usually difficult for balanced pleasurers. They don't mind organizing activities or taking the lead in relationships. Others also appreciate their fluidity and creativity. Personally, I find balanced pleasurers more engaging. They tend to do more, so they're great conversationalists and usually have interesting stories. Another thing that I've experienced with friends who are balanced pleasurers is that they let you talk and engage you in your own world more than either over- or under-pleasurers do.

6. Health

Most of the balanced pleasurers I've met are pretty healthy. I don't mean that they're marathon runners or obsessive calorie counters—they tend to consume their fair share of desserts, as do we all.

I find that overpleasurers tend to have accidents more than balanced pleasurers. I know a doctor who was an extreme overpleasurer. He had a skiing accident that laid him up for a month, then had another mishap because of not being totally healed from the first one.

Underpleasurers have stress buildup that's manageable in the early years, but it seems to catch up with them later. Although balanced pleasurers can get hit with pressure just like anyone else, my experience is that they're just physically more active and healthier.

There's always more to be said, but I think you're getting the general idea that moving toward being a balanced pleasurer is a good idea. People who can harness the power of pleasure in their lives are going to have more real enjoyment all-around. They can keep a balanced triangle of relationships, responsibility, and pleasure.

You deserve the journey! As you hike through the next pages, you'll be able to identify your pleasure zones appropriately. Then you'll have the chance to create a pleasure hierarchy and make plans to satiate your particular pleasure palate.

You're entitled to the power of pleasure. You deserve to feel that life is fun, worth living, and enjoyable!

Chapter Eight

Your Pleasure History

Well, so far I haven't played the counselor much, but here I'm going to have you go back in time . . . yes, down memory lane. I know that every time I think about reflecting on my remembrances, that song plays in my head—those of you over 40 may know immediately which one I'm talking about. That's right: It was the younger Barbra Streisand singing "The Way We Were." Sorry—I just had to get that out of my system before my pen would move on.

As a counselor, I often have to go backward to go forward. When clients talk to me about a current dysfunctional behavior in a relationship or their marriage, often— and I mean *really* often—it's the product of imprinting or learning that occurred during their childhood.

For one woman named Tammy, this early imprinting had horrific implications. Tammy was a pharmacist in her late 20s and the mother of three children: two daughters and a son. Her husband, James, was a good man who had a steady office job.

Tammy had few problems overall except her parenting, which was out of control. She was constantly spanking and yelling at her older daughter, Jessica. Even she felt that she was overcorrecting and her punishments were out of proportion compared to any of Jessica's behavior.

As Tammy and I went down memory lane, we gained quite a bit of insight. Tammy was an only child. Her mom had been a factory worker and her dad worked as a fireman. Tammy's mom was verbally and physically abusive to her. She recounted many occasions of having her hair pulled, being hit with brushes, and getting beaten senseless for little things.

Tammy went further back and recalled that her mother had also been the only daughter in her family and that *her* mother was raised in an orphanage. Beatings were so common there that it wasn't a question of *if* someone would get a beating that day, it was a question of *who* would get one.

So Tammy didn't know how to treat her first daughter any differently—this was imprinted and learned behavior. She didn't have the same reactions with her second daughter or her son, since she had no paradigms or imprinting for them. Tammy did get better quickly, as she really loved Jessica and didn't want to be the mother that *her* mother was. She made better choices (getting help, for example), and she was on her way.

Now, not only can negative imprinting or learning impact our current lives, so can positive imprinting. For example, Cochran was a handsome 42-year-old African-American man who was married with three boys. He was well adjusted, considering his past. You see, his dad died at an early age, and his mom didn't remarry until Cochran had started college.

Cochran spent a lot of time with his very spiritual, fun, and financially stable grandfather. Grandpa Ellis had a particular love for the ocean, which was only a short distance from where they all lived. Every Saturday Cochran would spend time with him.

Cochran loved his grandpa. They talked about life, God, girls, and money and told each other all kinds of stories while Grandpa Ellis painted the ocean, the board-walk, or some other scene close to the beach. He would paint two or three hours and then they'd go home, where Grandma Ellis always had a good lunch for her "boys."

In his junior-high-school years, Cochran would also paint regularly with his grandpa, and he actually regretted leaving the beach to go to college. Once he had his own family, he still got out his palette in a spare room over-looking the mountains in Colorado Springs and talked to God, his sons, or his beautiful wife as he painted. He loved to paint and talk. Even though Grandpa Ellis had passed away many years ago, it was as if he were alive, providing comfort, conversation, and creativity while Cochran created his pictures in his upstairs room with the mountain view.

Cochran's and Tammy's stories aren't unique. I haven't met a single person whose past doesn't have something to do with the present. As we study the history of ourselves, we can make choices not to repeat certain patterns and to continue with ones that have proven successful.

People who were fortunate enough to grow up in a family where saving money was valued are blessed. Their moms and dads took the time to teach them the basic lesson of "If you keep working and saving, you can afford purchases in the future." This is a great example of building something positive from the past and maintaining it because it works.

I'm going to take you on an intentional and educational walk down *your* memory lane. This is no ordinary stroll because we only want to focus on your pleasure history. You're going to fill out which types of pleasure occurred in each major zone—body, soul, and spirit—for different age categories.

This memory-lane walk will require a writing instrument and a separate piece of paper or journal. (For those of you who prefer a word processor, you can turn on your computer and fill out the same categories there.) This stroll will be very important in later chapters, so please take the time to review your pleasure history. You'll learn much about your particular pleasure zones that can help you harness the power of pleasure in your current life. Like Cochran, you may find that there's a little of the spirit of Grandpa Ellis alive in you!

Learning about your history of pleasure can truly be an enriching experience. As I've said throughout this book, you're worthy of the best pleasure possible, and sometimes that just means maintaining what has already proved to work for you in the past.

On your piece of paper or in your journal, write down examples where they belong in the following pleasure categories. Copy the chart for each five years of life (that is, ages 5–9, 10–14, 15–19, and so on up to your current age). As you go through your history, it will be normal not to have all pleasures in all ages. I want you to pen examples you've actually experienced, so take your time on this stroll.

Pleasure History

Body Pleasures

1. Sight Pleasure:
2. Touch Pleasure:
3. Taste Pleasure:
4. Hearing Pleasure:
5. Smell Pleasure:

Soul Pleasures

1. Humor Pleasure:
2. Risk Pleasure:
3. Calm Pleasure:
4. Spending Pleasure:
5. Travel Pleasure:
6. Integrity Pleasure:
7. Giving Pleasure:
8. Sex Pleasure:
8. Relationships Pleasure:
9. Creativity Pleasure:

Spirit Pleasures

1. Meditation Pleasure:
2. Prayer Pleasure:
3. Service Pleasure:

❧

I hope that you allowed yourself the time to go through your pleasure history. If you didn't, I really encourage you to reconsider and grab your writing utensil again.

However, if you really did a pleasure history for the first time in your life, congratulations—you worked hard. You might want to review what you wrote over the next day or so to make sure that it's as complete as you'd like it to be.

History gives you a foundation to build on in the future. As you read the next chapter, you'll gain an awareness of what you've already experienced as far as pleasure goes. Deciding to maintain those pleasures is part of the task before you.

History also gives you insight into what you might not have experienced yet as far as pleasure in your life. This is especially true if you come from a family where a particular pleasure wasn't available or encouraged. For instance, your family might not have valued calm, integrity, prayer, or risk, so your history might have significant absences in those pleasure zones.

This part of your past will also be something for you to look at. You may decide not to experience a particular area of pleasure. On the other hand, you might want to experiment with some pleasures that you haven't really tried. There may be a color that hasn't been used in your palette of pleasure. When you add it, it may make a significant positive difference in your life.

Right now I'm thinking of my wife, Lisa. Lisa is, of course, an absolutely wonderful lady, and every day I'm grateful to be married to her. She's primarily a calm, soul-pleasure person. Her idea of a perfect vacation would include looking at scenery, relaxing, and enjoying time with the children and me. By nature, she isn't a big risk person.

I'll never forget one summer when we spent some time in Vail, Colorado. (When you live in Colorado you can drive to these beautiful places.) We stayed at a nice hotel and picked up some brochures. One of them advertised a camp near a lake surrounded by mountains, with horseback riding, canoeing, and several other activities, including zip-lining—climbing at least 50 feet up a tree and gliding down in a harness to another, 20-foot tree.

I'm all about risk, as are both my children, so we talked Lisa into doing a zip line. Now the distance between the two trees was just short of 200 feet, so the glide lasted for quite a while. I went, then Hadassah, then Jubal, and finally it was Lisa's turn. She stood there: She didn't want to climb back down, and she didn't want to jump off that perfectly good tree either. She asked the guy helping us to push her so that she could zip down to the other side. Rarely has she screamed so loud—of course, as a family we still chuckle at this. Lisa experimented, and jumping from trees is permanently off her list.

More than a year ago we bought a couple of all-terrain vehicles. At first, Lisa was okay with this "for the children." However, when she got on a four-wheeler, she became the "motorcycle mama." She now wants to race, does all kinds of reasonable risky maneuvers, smiles, and laughs. She's truly a free spirit . . . it's like nothing else she's ever done in her entire life.

So Lisa experimented in two ways. Going on a zip line led to the conclusion that such a level of risk was absolutely not pleasurable for her. However, the four-wheeler experience is a lifelong addition to Lisa's repertoire of pleasure. Just yesterday, she suggested that we go up to the mountains and four wheel with the children. Next week we'll be somewhere in Colorado with "motorcycle mama" having the time of our lives and enjoying the power of pleasure as a family.

I want to congratulate you on your journey down memory lane. I hope that you've seen much that's given you pleasure and created a map of where you might need to experiment to tap into some new pleasures for yourself.

You're now in a place of greater understanding of how your current pleasure palette has evolved. Now the brush to paint your own lifestyle of pleasure is clearly in your hands!

ꗞ ꗞ ꗞ

Chapter Nine

Your Hidden
Pleasure Hierarchy

S o much of life is figuring out the "system" to see how
things work. Once we do (which can take years), we
move through that area of life much more quickly.

I remember working on my master's degree and becoming very frustrated. All I knew about school was that you
signed up for your classes, bought your books, got your
syllabus on the first day, and off to the races you went. I
was newly married and working at least 40 hours a week.
Then midterms would come along, or else all the papers
would be due the week of finals. These marathon weeks
were very hard on me and sometimes stretched my physical and mental capacities as well as consumed my time.

I remember thinking that there must be a better way . . .
another system. What I didn't know was that there was
actually a *hidden* system. Once I discovered and worked
it, my life improved greatly. I became a better student and
had much less stress in my life when I applied it to the
rest of my academic career.

Here's the hidden system I discovered:

1.   Figure out the classes you want to take the
     following semester.

2.   Find out the names of all the professors who
     teach the classes.

3. Go to the professors' offices, ask them or their secretary for the syllabus, and inquire if there will be many changes to it for the next semester.

4. Compare all of the professors who teach the same class.

5. Choose the one who requires the least amount of work.

6. Last and most important, complete as much of the work on the syllabus as you can before you start the class.

I couldn't believe how many times one professor would ask for almost double the workload that another required for the same number of credits. I saved many hours not writing 10- to 15-page papers when the professor I chose only asked for 5-page ones. I loved finishing a whole course, including book reports, readings, and papers, before sitting in the chair on the first day of class.

I even had fun sometimes asking if I could turn work in early. I'd pull out the entire course and hand it over. You should have seen the look on my professors' faces. They knew that I'd discovered the hidden system. Once I did, school was a piece of cake for me. It's true that while my friends were goofing off, I was working like crazy, but I always saw them scramble to catch up later in the semester. They would ask me about this paper or that assignment, and I'd just say, "Oh, I had that completed before class started." They stared at me as if I must have been joking. Although I shared this hidden system with them, to my knowledge nobody I went to school with utilized the information.

Hidden systems are all around us. Many areas such as real estate, welfare, and grant writing have lots of them. As I was listening to the radio a while back, the host talked about a Website that helps people navigate the phone-answering processes of large corporations in order to shorten the time it takes to actually speak to a real person. Finding the hidden system and utilizing it makes life easier, less draining, and more fun. I remember feeling so energized while doing my schoolwork with no pressure—it was great.

You may be wondering why I'm bringing this up. What does all this hidden-system talk have to do with harnessing the power of pleasure in your life? *Everything* is my answer.

Let me introduce you to Dean, an educated man who was a general superintendent of a large school district. Dean was experiencing headaches, sleepless nights, and marital stress. He also had two teenage sons, one of whom was in high school in the district where Dean was superintendent at the time.

Dean was a classic underpleasurer. He worked harder and longer than he needed to. He had almost no friends who weren't just acquaintances at the office. He had few spiritual, political, or social activities to speak of, but he watched television quite frequently.

Dean was definitely burning out. He needed some help to get his life back. He felt like he was adrift on a raft going down the Mississippi River: aimless, not connected, and really not having fun.

Dean was able to try the exercise you did in the last chapter: He walked down memory lane. He was really surprised by what he discovered about himself. Before taking this walk, he thought that learning would have been a primary pleasure for him. He admitted that his parents were really the ones who made him go to college, and his school district had strongly suggested that to move up the ladder, he needed to continue in his education. He also realized that he hadn't read just to learn on his own for many years.

Dean was a quiet guy. He was slow to warm up to people, but once he did, he'd crack jokes and be more personable. As he walked down memory lane, he was able to see that he really didn't get that much out of the soul-pleasure zone. Even TV wasn't a source of entertainment; rather, he watched it as a default activity. His spiritual zone wasn't developed in his life at all. Although he had some mild interest, it really wasn't a pleasure zone for him either.

What Dean found out about himself was rather funny. He grew up in a small town in Alabama. Dean's parents were poor and so were most of the people he knew and went to school with.

The men in their neighborhood had a peculiar tradition. Since most of them were driving older cars, something on somebody's car always needed to be fixed, tuned up, or changed. Most of the guys were above-average mechanics. On hot summer nights, the men would hover around a car in the way that many women flock around a newborn baby. They had their ice teas, Cokes, snacks, and beer.

Although these men appeared to be tinkering with cars, really they were relating to each other. They'd talk about sports, their wives and kids, religion, politics, their dreams, and just about anything else that came up. If you were looking in from the outside, you'd think that these guys were just friends who had found an excuse to get out of the house and talk to each other without being disturbed.

As the boys in the community became young men, they too were introduced to this small-town Alabama tradition. They learned to change starters, pull plugs, adjust belts—and well, be a man. This is where the guys connected.

Dean had long ago moved away from Alabama, but he didn't leave that pleasure zone behind. He still enjoyed tinkering and chatting at the same time. He was really kinesthetic and loved to work with his hands.

Once Dean realized what his hidden pleasure hierarchy was, he started on a new path. After I prodded him to see if he knew anybody who worked on cars, owned a repair shop, or had a similar hobby, Dean remembered that his cousin (who had the same upbringing) had called him more than a year ago asking him to help him with a kit car he'd purchased.

His cousin had a great garage, but after all this time, he'd barely even gotten the tires on the car. So after some encouragement from me, Dean asked his cousin if the two of them could work on the car together. The next week, they started on it.

When Dean talked about his new pleasure and project, he beamed like a schoolboy. He went on and on about it. He'd found his hidden pleasure zone. He had a few others to put in place as well to become a balanced pleasurer. Dean's symptoms of stress just flat-out disappeared. You see, Dean needed a car friend, and he was on his way to utilizing the power of pleasure in his life.

Your hidden pleasure might not go as far back as Dean's did. However, your history can give you great insight into your hidden pleasure hierarchy. Discovering it can make it easier for you to design a practical plan in the following chapters to make the power of pleasure work for you.

Let's begin with the major areas of pleasure: body, spirit, and soul. In each one, I want you to identify some major pleasure themes. Take information from your pleasure history in the last chapter and see if you can discover a hidden hierarchy of pleasure.

On a separate piece of paper or in a journal, please list the major body, soul, and spirit pleasure themes in the following age categories that apply to you. Identify the ones that you've experienced over your lifetime. You're just starting with some basic themes that can help you see the broad spectrum of pleasure over the decades. (Note that the soul has many pleasures and may go through various changes over time.)

- Ages 5–19
- Ages 20–39
- Ages 40–59
- Age 60+

The next step in finding your hidden hierarchy of pleasure is to reduce your thoughts down to a single impression. On a separate piece of paper or in a journal, I want you to succinctly write a theme for each major pleasure zone (body, spirit, and soul), using the statements below. Reducing everything down to a sentence can help you see clearly to the last step.

- My life experience with *body* pleasure tells me that _____.

- My life experience with *spirit* pleasure tells me that _____.

- My life experience with *soul* pleasure tells me that _____.

You're doing great. By now it's becoming clear where your pleasure hierarchy is located. Based on your pleasure hierarchy, pleasure themes, and your "reduction" statements, I want you to think about an important question: In which primary pleasure zone do you seem to experience the most pleasure—your body, your spirit, or your soul?

Now when I say to "think" about this question, I mean really *think*. You might want to take some time and sit on it for a day or so in order to process your answer. Most of us experience pleasure in all three primary pleasure zones . . . but which one really seems to be elevated above the other two for your unique personhood?

- I believe that my highest primary pleasure zone is my [body, soul, or spirit].

Let's continue this process with another question: Which pleasure zone do you believe is your second-highest primary pleasure zone? Is it your body, spirit, or soul?

- I believe that my second-highest primary pleasure zone is my [body, soul, or spirit].

By default, you've also identified your last primary pleasure zone. Which one is it?

- I believe that my third-highest primary pleasure zone is my [body, soul, or spirit].

On a separate piece of paper or in a journal, write out your primary pleasure zones in order. Place a 1 by the highest, a 2 by the second highest, and a 3 by the third highest.

You now know your hidden pleasure hierarchy.

Congratulations! In a later chapter, this information will really help you be the architect of a behavioral plan to unleash the power of pleasure in a new way. Discovering your highest primary pleasure zone is like finding the right sleep number on your air-bed mattress or figuring out a vitamin that works best for you. From here you can build a life of pleasure.

Before we move on, I want to give a little more substance to your building blocks of pleasure. This can help you in the next chapter when you move toward pleasure lifestyle planning.

On a separate piece of paper or in a journal, make a list of specific activities that are pleasures for you, starting with your highest pleasure zone and moving on to your second and third highest. All I want you to do in this section is brainstorm. (The pleasures in each category don't need to be in any specific order.)

Some of your pleasures may be time-consuming. Take kayaking, for instance: This activity is a half- or whole-day event unless you live right on the waterfront of a lake, river, or ocean. Unfortunately, due to time, money, or location, you might not be able to do some of your favorite pleasure zones as often as you like.

I can really relate to this. I love white-water rafting. This hits so many of my pleasures: friends, family, water, exercise, and the great outdoors. Unfortunately, it's a two-hour drive to get to the river, a four-hour event, and then a two-hour drive back. It takes all day, which is the reason why I do it less frequently than I might wish to.

It's very okay and normal for us to have bigger and more time-consuming activities that bring us pleasure. Of course, a calm-pleasured person only needs a few moments of peace and quiet, but even that can sometimes be almost impossible on a sunny day with so many children in the neighborhood and adults who like to do loud yard work. Limitations are part of life, and we often have to work around them.

Therefore, I also want you to brainstorm smaller-scale activities in your primary pleasure zones. These are pursuits that could take 15 to 30 minutes, a time allotment that's much easier for most of us to fit into our schedule.

I might not be able to go white-water rafting between seeing clients, but I *can* walk 30 minutes along the small creek across the street from my office. I could do this a couple times a week and bring significant added pleasure into my life during the year.

On a separate piece of paper or in a journal, I'd like you to write out short, doable activities in your highest, second-highest, and third-highest primary pleasure zones.

🌷

You've completed enough work in this chapter to help launch you into the fun world of pleasure. You've walked down memory lane and taken the fruit of your past and organized a potentially delightful present and future.

Speaking of the future, there's something fun you can do with your hidden hierarchy. So far we've talked about the past and present pleasures we've already been exposed to. That's great, but what about the ones we haven't experienced yet?

When it comes to pleasure, most of us have lived on an island, so to speak. We have our limited perspectives based upon our limited "island" experience. Now let's take the ferry off the island and go to the city of pleasure, where there are activities you have yet to experience in all the primary pleasure zones.

Not every place you go in this city will bring a pleasure that you'll want to permanently integrate into your repertoire of pleasure. However, even if you only discover a few new activities that add something enjoyable to your life, it's worth the ticket to get on the ferry, cross the waterway, and potentially encounter some new pleasures.

So again I want you to brainstorm. List possible activities that you'd be open to trying. If you can't think of any, ask friends or family for help. You can also just flip through the yellow pages to come up with ideas for future pleasures. On a separate piece of paper or in a journal, write these brainstorming ideas in the order of your pleasure hierarchy.

❦

Well, you've traveled quite a bit in this chapter. You've gone into the past for insight into the present, and left the present to create a more pleasurable future. You're a trooper!

This has been a fun trip. Like a guide on a white-water rafting trip, I've gone down this river so many times that it's as familiar as the back of my hand. Yet every time I go, it's somehow new and fresh to me. Your adventure is in many ways just beginning. You'll be creating a new life with the power of pleasure and experiencing a greater pleasure lifestyle.

Pause, enjoy the fresh air, and put your proverbial paddle back in the water. There's more to see and do. Just stay on board for these next pages and row when asked to—I promise you that the views will be worth it!

❦ ❦ ❦

X-ing and
Double-dipping

Well, by now I'm sure that you're thoroughly convinced that you're made for pleasure! You have a really good idea of what your particular pleasure palette and hierarchy look like. You're aware of the power of pleasure and have great ideas about how to harness it in your life.

In this chapter, I want to add two ideas I call *X-ing* and *double-dipping.* Before we get into them, I want to introduce to you a couple of friends.

Betty was an energetic 42-year-old lady. She was active at her kids' school and in the women's league. She also played tennis regularly and kept up with several friends in her neighborhood. Betty was a pretty balanced pleasurer.

Betty also had a problem, and nobody knew how she felt about it. You see, Betty was brought up in the Northeast. In her family, "on time" meant being ten minutes early. Arriving at the appointed hour was to be late, and lateness was intolerable. She remembered her parents commenting on how people who were late for family functions, church, school, or any type of event were lazy, thoughtless, or selfish.

You guessed it: Betty was chronically late. She thought that she'd gotten her genes from one of her aunts on her mother's side who was so consistently late that the family would actually lie to her and tell her that events took place an hour earlier than they really did so that she'd arrive closer to on time.

Betty was late for doctors' appointments, picking up her children, tennis games, and even some dates with her husband. She didn't just laugh it off as some people do with their particular traits. She shamed herself, thinking, *You're irresponsible, selfish, and stupid.* She brooded over these events for days. She asked her husband for help, but he gave up after their third year of marriage and just took his own car so that he wouldn't also be late. This crushed Betty because her husband is a gentle soul. Betty needed to X or double-dip to get a better handle on this. We'll continue with Betty in a little bit.

Karl was a great guy overall. He was a computer-software engineer, and he mountain biked regularly (his physical pleasure zone). He also loved—and I mean *loved*—chocolate ice cream. And not just any kind would do . . . it had to be Breyers chocolate ice cream (his specific taste pleasure zone). He also had an active family life and was involved with the men's group in his spiritual community.

Now overall, Karl was a pretty healthy guy and a balanced pleasurer. He smiled a lot, but privately he had a nagging issue that bothered him at least daily: He was 30 pounds overweight.

He said that he felt like the "fat guy on the bike." He'd tried several diets. He almost started to cry as he was talking to me about this. We set up a double-dip, and he was able to shed 19 pounds pretty quickly.

Now in my clinical experience, people find motivation both in increasing and in withholding pleasure. For some individuals, adding an extra day of pleasure really piques their interest, and they want to know where to sign up. For others, forgoing a pleasure for a short time can create motivation.

Let's take the primary pleasure zone of golf, which is as much social as it is physical. For one golfer named Tim, adding an extra nine holes to his game would be like going to heaven, regardless of how regularly he was able to practice. For Gerald, another golfer, not playing on Saturday would be so painful that he'd almost be beside himself for a week.

X-ing

As a writer, I often send a perfectly good manuscript to a publisher's editor. Now I must admit that occasionally my sentence structure lacks perfection, and other times it's probably awful.

Regardless of how wonderful I think the manuscript is, the editor's job is to find something wrong. You know what I mean? It's kind of like an IRS auditor. Even if you were pretty meticulous about the way you prepared your taxes, it's actually that person's job to find something you missed or did wrong, which is what these very fine editors do with my manuscripts.

In the early days before all the e-mail and attachments, this was done by hand. So when I received the manuscript back, it would have these little—and sometimes large—red (they always used red) Xs all over my wonderful, clean manuscript.

This "X-ing" of pleasure is the way some people find motivation to change. By X-ing a pleasure to modify behavior, they set up a kind of game. Now I caution you on this one: Only make the game last two months.

The "X" game goes like this: If I do something that I'm trying to change, I'll X out, or give up, a primary pleasure. When people are X-ed in a primary pleasure zone, it really hurts and gets their attention.

Let's make this a little bit more practical in its application. Remember "I'm always late" Betty? She struggled with this problem forever, but in six weeks and three X-ings, she was on time more often than she'd ever been before.

What Betty did was attach her goal of being on time to a major pleasure zone. You see, before she was just feeling bad, and other people would give her the same disappointed look that she remembered her parents giving her. Although it was painful for her to experience being late to another event, her pain wasn't felt in the right spot.

So Betty attached her goal to a pleasure zone. Betty's primary pleasure was tennis, which she played regularly. She was always in the top two spots at her country club, which was consistently ranked in the top six in the city.

Betty had played tennis since she was 12 years old and took lessons at the country club in her hometown. This pleasure zone was *very* important to Betty, especially when she was involved in leagues and tournaments.

So I proposed that Betty connect her habit of being late with tennis. If she was late (more than three minutes), she couldn't play tennis for three days, regardless of her tournaments or leagues.

She looked petrified about this at first, but she really wanted to change. She replied, "It's only for two months, right?" She was relieved, even though she knew that the X-ing was going to really hurt, especially if it extended over a weekend.

Betty did really well for ten days, and then she was seven minutes late picking up her children. She kept her word and gave up tennis, but she was really impacted. She went 14 days after that without being late and then another 6 days, after which she didn't have another lapse until she stopped the experiment. She started to enjoy her budding reputation for not being the last one to arrive.

Betty was happy with her results because she was able to end a behavioral struggle by utilizing the knowledge she had about her pleasure. Not only was she able to harness it, but she directed it like a laser beam to break out of a pattern that was causing her real pain.

Double-dipping

Karl, on the other hand, had tried withholding all the pleasurable things he could think of to motivate himself to drop the 30 pounds he was disgusted about. However, he needed an entirely different strategy that worked with his primary motivation style. You see, deep down, Karl worked much more on the basis of reward than he did upon threat of punishment. He had a unique way of shutting down and not caring if he didn't get to watch the game or do a certain thing.

So as Karl was working on this, he used his pleasure hierarchy. His primary pleasure zone was taste. As I mentioned before, he liked chocolate—most of all, chocolate Breyers ice cream. Now rewarding himself with this treat in order to lose weight seemed odd at first, but Karl was convinced it might work. (Remember, I told you how creative and fluid balanced pleasurers are.)

Well, Karl wanted to surprise me with his plan, and indeed he did. He came back with a solution to lose his dreaded weight.

He moved his morning bike riding to 6 P.M., with his wife's cooperation. He made a guideline: No sugar or food of any kind afterward, and he had to be in bed no later than 9 P.M. This was a drastic change because at night Karl sat in front of the television or computer. The later he stayed up, the more food he consumed, and this was the time he'd usually had his scoop of Breyers ice cream.

"This plan looks great," I said, "but where is the pleasure—you know, the reward you needed?"

He smiled like a Cheshire cat, knowing that he baited me into asking the question he wanted me to. He said sheepishly, "I'm going to double-dip."

"Double-dip?" I asked. "What do you mean?" Again, he knew that he was stringing his therapist along like a mouse following a piece of cheese connected to a string through a maze.

"You're aware that I like Breyers chocolate ice cream, right? Well, you also may or may not know that my office is only a few minutes from my home, so I go there for lunch every day."

I bent forward in my chair, waiting for the magic solution.

He continued, "So I'll weigh myself in the morning, and if I weigh less than I did before, even a quarter of a pound, I get two dips—a double-dip—of chocolate ice cream at lunch. I figure that if I eat it during the day, I can burn it off. I'll feel victorious rather than like a failure. What I don't burn off during the day, I'll burn off with my bike ride. If I don't eat anything or drink sugary sodas afterward, I won't have calories turning into fat at night while I sleep. Also, by going to bed early, my metabolism will still be up from the bike ride, and I won't be snacking on a thousand calories before sleep anymore."

Karl was so proud of his plan. I think that he was also excited that he came up with it himself and could keep me in suspense during the session.

As funny as it seemed, his plan worked, since Karl utilized a very high pleasure zone for himself. He meticulously weighed in every morning, and for the most part kept to his plan. In a two-month period—the length of his experiment—he lost 19 pounds.

What about Me?

That's right—what about you? Like the rest of us, are you a flawed but loved human being who has a behavior you want to change? Would you like to be like Karl and Betty and take the power of pleasure, actually aim it at something, and see if it can help remove a habit that's been plaguing you?

I know that when I direct the power of pleasure at something, I see incredible results. I remember that early in our marriage, Lisa and I were talking about something that I really didn't like—being in debt. We didn't really owe that much: Both our cars were paid off and so were all my student loans.

What I didn't like was our mortgage. I really wanted to be debt free, so I used the power of pleasure to help me with this problem. Similar to Karl, I like rewards more than punishment. I enjoy feeling as if I beat something and won.

So I talked to Lisa—or rather, I made a deal with her. We got our budget together, which included dates and vacations, and we agreed on a monthly amount. Any dollar over that would go toward the principal on the mortgage.

141

You're probably thinking, *So what's the pleasure in that?* Well, here's where the deal got sweet for me: When we achieved freedom from debt, I could buy a significant "toy" for myself.

I don't think Lisa really believed that this could happen, so she agreed to this condition. All I needed was a carte blanche to buy my toy—once we started, it was amazing how much money came from different directions: book sales, conferences, and a steady practice. It took a little more than a year, and the power of pleasure kept me motivated to pay off a sizable amount of the mortgage.

Yes, I know that some of you are curious . . . I did buy my toy. Getting rid of the debt was just an obstacle to my pleasure, so it was a done deal. You see, the power of pleasure sustained me and let me keep aiming at something that I wanted removed from my life.

I know that this way of using the power of pleasure might be a new approach for you. I want to walk you through the basic steps of this process. Then you can decide whether or not to try to utilize the power of pleasure to help you with a struggle in your life.

Let's talk for a second. Pretend you're coming to my office. Have a seat, and get nice and comfortable. After some pleasantries, I ask you a question you haven't thought about.

I point to the small wand sitting on the table that's comfortably situated between us, and I ask, "If this were a magic wand that I could wave over you, and a negative behavior or something you didn't like about yourself could be changed, what would it be?"

What would you say? No, seriously . . . take a minute, even if you have to close the book and stop reading. Be honest—most of us have something.

On a separate piece of paper or in a journal, complete this statement: "My behaviors I wish to be changed are _____."

You took the first step, which in AA they say can often take the longest. All of us are flawed but loved humans who have some annoying trait to be reined in. So if you'd like to see fewer of these behaviors in your life, keep being honest, and by all means keep reading.

Now I need you to reflect a little bit on your life. I want you to guess if you're more motivated by withholding a pleasure (X-ing) or by adding pleasure (double-dipping).

Take a moment and decide which of the following best describes you:

- **X-ing:** I am more motivated by withholding a pleasure from myself (for example, by not playing golf, seeing a girlfriend, getting a massage, or buying a new toy).

- **Double-dipping:** I am more motivated by increasing my pleasure (for example, more time for golf or friends, an extra massage, or a new toy).

All right, you're making some real progress here. Now let's identify your core pleasures. On a separate piece of paper or in a journal, I just want you to list your top two or three pleasures in each major area of your being—body, soul, and spirit.

Which of these would probably be your two highest pleasures? It's acceptable if they're both in one area of your being (soul, body, spirit). On a separate piece of paper or in a journal, record what your two highest pleasures are.

Now we come to a very important part of harnessing the power of pleasure—brainstorming. Brainstorming is when you just let any and all combinations exist without concern for practicality, right or wrong, or personal preferences. You're just coming up with ideas on how to connect the behavior you want diminished to a pleasure of yours. So on your separate piece of paper or in your journal, write down a few ideas that might be options. (You can label them *Option 1, Option 2,* and so forth.)

- If I participate in _____, I'll X _____.

- If I don't participate in _____, I'll double-dip _____.

We're definitely getting closer. Take a few minutes, or even a day or so if you need to. Now if any of your ideas affect others (such as *I won't take a shower*), then get the consent of those who might be impacted prior to committing to them. Write out your best idea, and record your plan to harness pleasure to help you eliminate an unwanted behavior from your life.

The Next Step

The next thing you might want to do that I've found very helpful is to buy a writing tablet or use your journal to keep a record of your progress. If you blow it, be honest. This journal can help you when you feel like quitting, and it also lets you see your positive movement over time.

A great thing to do to facilitate your success is to buddy up—that is, involve a friend, preferably someone of the same gender. Let him or her know what your game plan is and what you're working on.

Check in with your friend a few times a week to let him or her know your progress. If you slip, be truthful, and make sure you report how your X-ing or double-dipping is going—this allows you to stay honest. I find that clients who involve another person in their harnessing of the power of pleasure to remove a behavior are more likely to stay on course and stick to their plan.

On your writing tablet or in your journal, write the names of the buddy (or buddies) whom you'd most likely involve in this process.

There's one last thing that you have to decide on, since you've already established *What?* (that is, the unwanted behavior), *How?* (X-ing or double-dipping), and *Who?* (your buddy). Now all that's left is *When?* That's right, when would you like to harness the power of pleasure to change yourself? So as soon as you're ready, write out a date when you want to start your plan.

Just for review purposes, I'm going to briefly outline the process of harnessing the power of pleasure to help with difficult behaviors.

Harnessing the Power of Pleasure
to Help with Unwanted Behaviors

1. Identify the unwanted behavior.

2. Figure out your motivation (X-ing or double-dipping).

3. Identify your pleasure.

4. Brainstorm.

5. Create your plan.

6. Journal your progress.

7. Buddy up with someone.

8. Establish a start and end date.

As you repeat this process again and again, it gets to be really fun. I've been able to diminish my unwanted behaviors, and I've seen many people such as Karl and Betty achieve great results in their lives. So utilize X-ing and double-dipping as often as you want.

The power of pleasure is always available. For the honest soul, there's usually *something* that can be improved. Take your time and only work on one behavior at a time. You can become a better you for yourself and for those you love—and the power of pleasure is definitely one way to get there!

🌷 🌷 🌷

Chapter Eleven

Giving Pleasure to Others

William Booth, the founder of the Salvation Army, which is a great social and spiritual organization, was confronted with a serious financial crisis. He was urged by those closest to him to write a letter to his previous supporters.

He might have been pressured to write a compelling letter about how much money was needed in order to make ends meet. He could have gone on and on about the good they were doing. Like many organizations today, he could have filled the letter with the stories of desperation or of people whose lives were changed because of the Salvation Army.

Booth, however, took a totally different approach to asking his constituency for help. He took up his pen and boldly wrote only one word: *others*. He sent the letter out, and the organization was generously supported through this very difficult time.

I'm telling you this story because although you're designed to receive pleasure, you're also designed to give it. So far in these pages, we've focused on how you're made for pleasure. By now you know your pleasure hierarchy and have plans to utilize the power of pleasure in your life. In this chapter, I want to highlight your ability to give pleasure to others.

So often we can get caught up in the busyness of our lives, including our tasks, agendas, and appointments. It's easy to take our eyes off of our potential for giving pleasure away, but we all have this ability. How have you been touched recently by a person saying or doing something that brought you pleasure?

I'm writing now on my way back from a conference. During the day, two much older women and one who was around my age were approaching the same door that I was walking toward. I did what any person who has manners would do: I opened the door wide and smiled at these ladies.

It must have been a while since someone opened a door for them. They looked first at each other and then at me before smiling and saying thanks. I know that it wasn't a big deal, but my gesture seemed to have brought them pleasure.

Four Ways You're Designed to Give Pleasure

Let's go ahead and dive into the different ways you're designed to give pleasure. For our discussion, I want to focus on four major methods.

1. Words

Your words are one of the most powerful forces you possess. The spoken word has the power to build people up and give them pleasure, as well as to destroy them and zap their pleasure. Just look at the following list, and I think that you'll get the point:

You're so smart.	You're so stupid.
You can do anything.	You can't do anything.
You're capable.	You're incapable.

You can easily feel the strength of the words in the left column, along with the pain of those in the right column—especially if you've heard them before.

In addition to receiving some of our greatest pleasures from words, many of us have been wounded by them. I myself come from a pretty neglectful background, so I'll never forget an incident that turned into a life-changing event for me.

Lisa and I had been married about four years or so, and we were getting ready to go to bed. She gently leaned over to me, gave me a kiss on the cheek, and said, "I love you." For whatever reason, those three words channeled through my body in a powerful way. I rolled over to her and asked wonderingly, "You really do, don't you?" She said yes, smiled, and went to sleep.

Even though I knew by her behavior that she loved me, the words really entered my heart. I was pleasured by the words of my lover and friend.

I want you to take a moment and consider how you use the power of your words. Think first in terms of your primary relationship with yourself and your spouse or significant other, parents, children, and deity. Are your words mostly encouraging; or are they rough, critical, and sarcastic? For an illustration, here's a way to look at it: If your words were fruit, what would others taste from you? You can pause and think about this, but it's critical in a pleasure lifestyle to give good fruit to all people and especially to those closest to you.

Then journey down and examine your secondary relationships: that is, your friends, co-workers, and neighbors.

What kind of fruit are *they* getting from you? Then look at the acquaintances and strangers you meet—what about them?

If you question how you're doing, keep track just for fun sometime. Take a piece of paper and record the negative words you're speaking on one side and the encouraging words on the other. You might be surprised by how the experiment turns out. Either way, you do have the power to positively impact others, so I encourage you to use words regularly as part of your lifestyle of pleasure.

2. Acts

Since you're designed to give pleasure, your behavior or actions can mean so much to others. That hug you gave or the thoughtful deed you did for someone just because you wanted to can make a difference.

I'm on my way back from a professional conference training I spoke at in Pennsylvania. The conference itself went well, but I want to share what happened that was so unusual.

A man showed up who lived two hours away. He'd come to counsel with me in Colorado Springs for a 3-Day Intensive (a workshop sponsored by my office, the Heart to Heart Counseling Center) a while back. His life was changed by what had happened to him there, and he subscribed to one of our free weekly e-mail newsletters. He found out that I'd be doing a conference in his area, so he came.

Although the conference was closed to the general public, the people who arranged it allowed the man to come in. He paid for his own room and asked for nothing. I was surprised to see him. He said to me, "I'll work at the book table, or if you need any errands done, I'm available. I'm here to help. " And he did just that. On the first day, he found out that due to flight delays, I didn't arrive until 4 A.M. He took it upon himself to get me an energy drink that took the edge off my exhaustion.

He acted with consistent kindness. He gave of himself, and this created amazing pleasure for me. When someone is considerate of you, you feel loved, respected, and valued.

We each have this ability to act with kindness, thoughtfulness, and caring toward others. We have to ask ourselves if we're consistently using our ability, especially in our primary relationships.

If your spouse, significant other, children, parents, and deity were put in a courtroom, what would they testify? Would they say that you regularly gave them pleasure? What about your secondary relationships—your friends, neighbors, or co-workers—what would they state about you? If the court needed further testimony from your acquaintances, what would be said?

Would there be enough facts and evidence to convict you of not pleasuring others? Would you be anxious as the jury deliberated? Would you have to plea-bargain because you're guilty?

Relax—court is not in session. Like Ebenezer Scrooge, most of us will have tomorrow to do better.

I personally love to surprise people with kindness. Being thoughtful is fun, whether it's to a clerk or to my family. I fail my fair share of the time, but I really like to give others the feeling of being respected and loved.

3. Money

I know that most of us feel that we don't have enough money. Some of us are living from paycheck to paycheck. Our thoughts about money sometimes don't evolve much. We may still act like a two-year-old who's been given a toy. The parents ask the toddler to share it with others, and the child speaks loudly enough to embarrass them: "Mine!" Mom and Dad appeal to the child once more, and again are met with the response: "No, mine!"

In all honestly, most of us can relate to our two-year-old friend. We can become self-focused at times, especially when it comes to money. However, money, like words and acts, is another way we're made to give pleasure to others. Most of us are affluent beings with financial resources. As Westerners, we're among the wealthiest people in world history. If all we do with our money is spend it on ourselves, we've missed out on a significant pleasure.

The joy of giving without expecting a return or a thank-you is one of the great pleasures of being human. I'm reminded of the story of a man who was driving a nice car. As he was pulling in to a gas-station parking lot, he saw a woman who had a grocery cart, the contents of which represented her belongings, and it looked like she was going to a Laundromat.

The woman walked into the convenience store. The man watched her as he pumped gas. He thought, *Oh great, I'm going to get hit up for some money when she comes out.* But that didn't happen. She quietly went in, got a soda, and continued on her way. As she started to leave, a young man nearby stopped her. He said, "Here, I'd like to help," and he gave her a $20 bill.

The woman was truly surprised as she looked at him and became tearful. The man watching thought about how much pleasure the young man had given her.

I'm sure that she walked away believing that there are good people, even good *young* people. I have a sense, however, that the woman wasn't the only one who felt pleasure. As the young man drove away, I'm sure that he was glad to have helped another person, especially someone who wasn't even asking for his assistance.

In this society, there are so many ways to give pleasure to others, including helping with the needs of individuals and giving to organizations that assist people or support ideas you believe in.

The pleasure of giving away resources is a great feeling. I've also found that people who do this don't usually brag or tell others. Rather, this pleasure is like a piece of chocolate that you let melt in your mouth in a quiet setting. It's sweet . . . so sweet.

If you haven't consistently tried giving the pleasure of resources to others, I'd strongly encourage you to start. Just find a needy person or organization and be generous. See how you feel, and imagine what the recipient might experience.

In Colorado Springs, there's a very large organization called Compassion International. We've all seen their commercials. They basically give you the opportunity to sponsor a specific underprivileged child from somewhere in the world. The child is fed, clothed, and even sent to school on your monthly gift.

Imagine being desperate, not knowing who your father or mother is or how you'll eat. You find out that someone around the world values you enough to care. I'm sure that you'd feel incredible pleasure and love.

4. Incorporating

By "incorporating," I'm not referring to tax identification or legal status for a company. What I mean can best be explained by a baking analogy.

You see, when you're making the best chocolate-chip cookies in the world, you have to "incorporate" during the entire process. You start with flour . . . then you incorporate white sugar, brown sugar, eggs, walnuts, chocolate chips, and a whole lot of other wonderful ingredients. All the components are innately different, but together, they make "music" that's as good as a philharmonic orchestra's symphony.

Incorporate means "to bring others into the mix." Be they your pleasures, responsibilities, or relationships, you bring them in—you incorporate them into your event, celebration, or relationships.

The pleasure that others receive in being incorporated is amazing, whether they're in a primary, secondary, or acquaintance relationship with you. Remember in grade school when teams were being selected for a game? As children, we liked to be thought of when someone was choosing whom to play with. All of us have said inside our hearts, *Pick me.* The pleasure we received in being selected is the joy of being incorporated into the game.

We each have within us the ability to give others pleasure by incorporation—by reaching out with a phone call or invitation of some kind. It's been a while since many of us have experienced the pleasure of being incorporated.

To watch even a professional, successful person beam when you say, "Hey, we're going here—why don't you come along?" is pleasurable. It's so fun that I encourage you to simply try it.

There are those who are just naturally good at giving this pleasure to others. These are the people who intuitively incorporate others. They usually have many friends, and in times of need they're usually very supported.

So if you haven't "incorporated" incorporating into your life lately, think of a person who might be pleasured by an invitation. You'll be amazed by how much your circle of friends can grow.

Two Principles

I want to discuss two principles that I see at work in the lives of those who learn to give pleasure to others. I share this so that you might be encouraged to follow their example as part of your own pleasure lifestyle.

1. Be Intentional

All of us are capable of the occasional kind word or deed. I call this "accidental fruit." If you're married or are in a primary relationship with a partner, you might be able to identify with the following example.

Your spouse or significant other is in a frenzy or funk and is being cross. Historically, you'd snap back, but for some reason you're patient instead. You lovingly detach (because you know that it's not about you) and respond with kindness, and your partner is helped and comforted by your reaction. You're as surprised as he or she is that you acted out of character on that occasion.

This was an accident. The days, weeks, and months that follow prove to be different. Your spouse or significant other provides you with other opportunities to give consistent fruit, and you, like most of us, fail miserably.

Here's an analogy. A farmer sits on his porch, and you curiously ask him what crop he's waiting for this year. He answers, "I don't have a clue . . . whatever comes up." You'd imagine that you were talking to a crazy person. You're thinking, *Doesn't he even grasp the basics? Everybody knows that you have to plant something so that you know what you'll get back.*

I have exactly the same thought when I see someone "planting" rudeness, lies, arrogance, self-importance, bitterness, or envy. What does that person really expect to get back?

The better way is to be intentional with pleasuring others. Set out to be kind to people and say encouraging words.

Right now I'm sitting in an empty theater where my children were just a part of a performance. (Yes, I actually do write books on planes, in empty theaters, and even while waiting at my kids' practices.) The performance was great, and the cast is backstage eating pizza and spaghetti (standard theater food). But where I am, an entirely different activity is occurring: There are 20-year-olds vacuuming and picking up all the trash from the performance, because there's another one in a couple of hours. I told one of these cleaners what a good job she was doing and how important her work was. She beamed and started to talk about her education. She appeared to feel acknowledged and encouraged.

I love doing this . . . I mean, I really do. I enjoy being a source of pleasure for others—whether they're businesspeople, clerks, cooks, waiters, my own staff, or my children's friends—by being positive. I intentionally want to uplift and encourage people.

Be intentional. Ask yourself, *Who in my various spheres of influence can I give pleasure to today?* Take a moment and think of someone in a primary, secondary, and acquaintance relationship. Then go plant a positive seed in these people's lives. That way, when someone approaches you one day and asks you, "So, what are you planting in the field of others' lives?" you have a much better answer than "I don't know . . . whatever comes up."

You absolutely deserve the joy that comes from an intentional harvest. I've met farmers who owned more than one county's worth of land. When you ask them what they're planting, the short answer is: "Over there— a hundred acres of wheat. In that direction are a hundred acres of barley, and down that way is corn. . . ."

They not only know what they've planted, they also know how to grow it, and they're aware that it will mature and be harvested. *You* also deserve to have such confidence in harvesting the seeds that you've intentionally planted over the years.

2. Expect the Harvest

If you give others pleasure, you can expect to see a harvest. When you plant, you really don't know when or how you'll reap what you've sown, but a harvest does come.

As I mentioned, I'm sitting in a theater that's being cleaned. What I didn't tell you was what happened at last night's performance. My children did well and were playing around after all the autographing was over, waiting for the adult cast members to decide where they wanted to eat.

The kids and young adults were playing Red Rover. In this game, a person runs from one team and tries to break through the line of the other team. If the runner bursts through their linked arms, someone from the other team goes back with him or her. My son, Jubal, ran with all his might into the strong arm of a very large adult male. His momentum caused him to bounce back and fall flat on his back, hitting his head. He couldn't feel anything in his limbs and was frightened. We ended up in the emergency room for hours. Thankfully, after x-rays and such, it was determined that he was fine.

A few members of the cast and crew came to the hospital and stayed with us until 2 A.M. Lisa and I were greatly touched by the harvest of support we received. This is an example of the second principle—finding a harvest after planting intentional pleasure in the hearts and lives of others.

I'm never surprised when good things happen to those who give others pleasure. I've heard hundreds of stories of unexpected kindness, opportunities, or connections to solutions involving people who regularly practice this.

Although you don't give pleasure to others expecting a reward or compensation of any kind, I've found that kindnesses happen. So as you're creating a lifestyle of pleasure for yourself and others, know that on so many levels, your life can be extremely positive and full of enjoyment. Be intentional in all your relationships, and smile when the pleasure comes back to you.

❀ ❀ ❀

Chapter Twelve

Your Daily Pleasure Appointment

One of the things I love about the recovery community is its slogans. These phrases have worked their way into mainstream culture, which I think is a good thing. Among the slogans I've enjoyed and passed on to many of my clients is "One day at a time."

Now for someone in recovery, this expression relates to abstaining from alcohol, drugs, sex, work, food, or whatever the person is addicted to. However, I like to use "One day at a time" as a principle for pleasuring.

Think of every day as an opportunity for pleasure. Pleasure surrounds us in the air we breathe, the colors we see, the sounds we hear . . . and yes, in the people we meet. It's everywhere all the time, so why not enjoy it today?

Think about it: We all have the same amount of time in a day, whether we're single or married with children. We all get the same 24 hours—the same 1,440 minutes.

Now here's where pleasuring daily comes in. You can easily look at your Palm Pilot, your day planner, or the scrap of paper you keep your life on and see where your day goes. For some of you, eight hours is taken up by work. Then there's at least an hour and a half devoted to eating, plus the commute to and from work. If you're a student, there are also classes, part-time jobs, and friends.

Even retired people and stay-at-home parents have appointments, schedules, leagues, or events to attend. Those with children have the time committed to meal preparation, consumption, and cleanup; household chores; homework; going to and from school and special activities; and let's not forget baths and bedtime rituals, including that 20-minute snack at night.

All this time that we're given every day seems to get spent in all different directions. Picture a photograph of an average man or woman with time coming out of his or her ears, eyes, nose, and so on. That's often how most of us look as far as our own time is concerned.

Now, let's move on to a few basic principles so that you can pleasure every day. Then I want to share some short accounts of how people have learned to find pleasure daily.

Principle #1: Pay Yourself First

As many of us start making more money, we start to read motivational, self-help, and management books. I'm one of those people who gets pleasure from learning, so of course I like them.

In my past reading, some of these financial books kept repeating a principle or slogan again and again: *Pay yourself first.* The basic idea is that before you take care of your bills or other financial obligations, you set a portion of money aside. Some authors suggested that you put this money in a savings or investment account. Others said that this is your fun money to enjoy so that you don't mind working as much.

The authors who taught this principle for savings had an interesting perspective and recommended that you pay yourself 5 to 15 percent of your income. As you put this amount away regularly, you have capital to invest. Investments earn money, and eventually you work your way toward making as much money through investments as you do in a 40-hour-a-week job.

Here's the point to this principle: A little over time adds up to a lot if you're consistent. The same is true of having a pleasure lifestyle. If you experience a little pleasure every day, then you'll have a huge amount over the decades you get to live on this beautiful planet.

Now this doesn't have to be a large or even a primary-pleasure-zone pleasure. This principle doesn't mean you set aside hours a day to travel, work out, or meet new people. Rather, this daily pleasure usually takes only minutes. Many smaller pleasures can be under 5—and definitely under 30—minutes a day.

When I share this principle of paying yourself first, sometimes people ask, "Do you mean that the first thing I do each day is a pleasure?" That's not my point exactly, although I do know of many individuals who take this principle literally. For some people, the aroma and warmth (not to mention the caffeine) of coffee is one of the major reasons they get out of bed in the morning. I also know the 5 A.M. ritual of the runners, walkers, and bikers in my neighborhood. I see them as I enjoy the pleasure of walking my dog, Moses (who, by the way, has a primary pleasure zone of 5 A.M. walks as well).

Pleasuring first really works for some of us. However, it's not my goal for everyone to pleasure first thing in the morning. I'm old enough to know that some people wake up perky and glad to be alive (you know the type), singing or humming. Others are, shall we say . . . *challenged* in the waking-up department. They stumble through the showering and getting-ready process, and by the time they want to say good morning, it's time for lunch.

That's okay. Regardless of how you wake up, applying the "One day at a time" principle means that you'll dedicate a few minutes to pleasure. Let me give you a few examples.

Jaz, a 21-year-old student, was full of life. He was finishing up at college with a full load of 12 hours. He also worked three nights a week and all day Saturdays at a hip restaurant in downtown Denver.

He had a girlfriend, loved to hang out with friends, and was ranked pretty high on the unofficial Frisbee-golf circuit on campus. To meet Jaz—a 6'1", athletic, bright-eyed young man—you'd never guess his primary pleasure.

You see, Jaz wasn't always tall, dark, and handsome. Actually, he was quite the geek in junior high and high school. He enjoyed two things, and together they recharged him greatly: (1) poetry, both classic and contemporary; and (2) calm, especially by water. He was very reflective and was pretty much on the path to burnout before he created a daily pleasure for himself. Even after two weeks, he noticed that he was more himself than he'd been in a long time. He also reported that his girlfriend loved this side of him.

What did Jaz do? He got a couple of poetry books and put them in his backpack. He would grab a water bottle and sit in a quiet spot under a tree next to the river that runs through downtown Denver by his school. He said that most times he'd read for 10 or 15 minutes. Then he would just reflect for a few minutes and be on his way before breakfast.

Theresa was a retired and widowed woman who had little time to spare. She said, "People think that you get more time when you retire, but I'm busier than ever." She went through her list of volunteering, babysitting seven grandchildren, and dabbling in a little real estate here and there.

Theresa, like many people her age, often would do so much for others that she became quite the under-pleasurer. Although she made annual and monthly pleasure agendas, I was most intrigued by the daily activity that she chose consistently.

You see, she and her husband, Jack, used to play golf a lot. Theresa was actually pretty good, and five years before Jack passed away, he'd placed a hole in the back-yard for putting practice. Theresa decided to give herself the pleasure of hitting three to five balls a day in the morning or evening. She enjoyed doing this—her whole body just loved it. When she would talk about getting a ball in the hole, she was as excited as a football fan dis-cussing a Super Bowl touchdown. Putting golf balls took mere minutes and brought her enough pleasure daily that she could go back to all her other activities.

You see, it doesn't take much time, but it does require an awareness of pleasure and an understanding of how its power can greatly affect your daily life.

Principle #2: Pleasure Is a Principle

Pleasure is many things, but hopefully by now you truly understand that it's a principle, similar to that of sowing and reaping, saving for a rainy day, and so on. If you apply the principle, you get results. If you avoid it, you suffer consequences.

There are many principles in life that we all know about, such as eating right, exercising, saving, and being kind to others. Some of us are more "principled" and adopt them regardless of how we feel about them. It's always the same guys who are out running or are at the gym at 5 A.M.—that's how they apply the principle of exercise.

Having knowledge of principles isn't enough to benefit from them. We all know to save money, but many of us don't put aside enough to live on for even a few months. But when we obey or comply with a principle, we're rewarded.

However, so many of us who were raised in the '60s or later are often challenged by this idea. For these generations, it appears rigid, legalistic, needless, and insane to be principle based. Such people are governed by their feelings: If they feel like it, they do it; if they don't feel like it, they don't. Often this leads to the extremes of over- or underpleasuring.

Pleasuring daily is one of those principles that will bring benefits if you comply with it. It's like the men and women who do 200 sit-ups a day: They're the ones with the ripped abs.

However, pleasuring is fun, unlike those sit-ups if you aren't used to them. Not only that, reading this book will allow you to pinpoint your exact *type* of fun—whether it's poetry and calm, as Jaz enjoyed; or golf-ball hitting, Theresa's pleasure.

Now before we go one step further, let's agree on something. The power of pleasure can be yours—daily and for the rest of your life. Like a person in recovery, you can have a whole new life enjoying the power of pleasure. Decide on which of the following applies to you:

- I agree that pleasure is a principle that I want to harness in my life.

- I agree that pleasure may be a principle, but I don't want to harness the power of pleasure in my own life at this time.

Well, hopefully you agree with the first statement. Even if you don't want to harness the power of pleasure, please read on so that when you do want to, you'll clearly know how to go about it.

You deserve the power of pleasure in your life. Now let's go to the next principle.

Principle #3: Make a Plan

Shall we get practical now? Well, of course—that's the whole idea behind receiving the benefits of the power of pleasure, especially on a daily basis. On a separate piece of paper or in a journal, I want you to briefly list some of your pleasures in each zone that would take fewer than 30 minutes a day.

- Body Pleasures (for example, ice cream, push-ups, listening to music, being touched, or walking)

- Soul Pleasures (for example, talking to a friend, reading a novel, playing an instrument, laughing at jokes, or creating a painting)

- Spirit Pleasures (for example, reading inspirational material, meditating, listening to religious teachings, encouraging others spiritually, or preparing to serve in a spiritual capacity)

165

You are a unique pleasure machine. The examples above are just to help stimulate ideas. Finding pleasure can be as easy as savoring a chocolate bar, drinking hot tea, making a phone call, or writing a paragraph in your unpublished novel.

Now that you have some ideas, it's time to make a plan for pleasure. For some people this means committing to one act of pleasure a day, such as Theresa's hitting her three to five golf balls. For others, making a plan for daily pleasure entails more of a variety—for instance, one week they might emphasize a particular zone of pleasure, be it body, soul, or spirit. Some just mix it all up by putting a little of everything in a week. This approach might include one to three activities in any of the body, spirit, or soul areas. What do you think would work for you?

- I like to engage in the same pleasure activity daily.

- I prefer a different one each time.

- I enjoy just mixing it up.

So you know your daily pleasures and how you want to distribute them. Now, on a separate piece of paper or in a journal, write in a pleasure for yourself each day.

Next let's make a commitment. I find that if you put something in writing, it helps you keep your goals of pleasuring. Write: "I am committed to start the principle of daily pleasure on _____, 20___."

Principle #4: Execute Your Plan

You now have a plan and a commitment to starting it. Congratulations, you've probably never been closer to having a life of pleasure than you are today.

I want to encourage you to execute your plan. If all you do is make a plan and you don't carry it out, you get no results.

One of the best ways to follow through is to incorporate a friend. Tell him or her that you're committed to doing something fun just for yourself every day. Explain that you're going to let him or her know what the activity is on a regular basis. Traveling the path of pleasure is always better with a friend.

Another way to help you execute your plan is to keep track of it on a daily basis. Just put a dot or a checkmark to indicate whether you did your pleasure activity today.

You're worthy of daily pleasure. You deserve a lifetime of pleasuring. Both of these statements are true, and both are possible . . . one day at a time. Let's meet some people who've mastered daily pleasuring. I offer these stories because sometimes hearing what others do can generate ideas for you.

- **Amanda:** *I walk on the beach, and I like to close my eyes until I hear the water deep inside of me.*

- **Chris:** *I do a couple of my tae kwon do forms— it wakes me up and centers me.*

- **Matt:** *I drink a great cup of coffee and sit out on the porch and pet my dog.*

- **Georgette:** *I crochet at least 15 minutes a day. It makes me feel close to the person I'm going to give the finished product to. I keep my crocheting in my car so that I can do it almost anywhere.*

- **Tim:** *I go on the Internet to read the headlines from a few large papers.*

- **Heidi:** *I like to make people smile or laugh. I've been tracking this for almost four months and haven't missed a day. I really like it when I get one of my children to smile.*

- **Dan:** *It's my mountain bike. I hit the park every possible day for at least 15 to 30 minutes. I like the wind and the concentration, and the sweat's not so bad either.*

I've seen people really change with some daily pleasure in their life. Pleasure seems to be like the oil in the engine of life. Those people whose life is lubricated just seem to purr along as opposed to sputtering, overheating, and being less functional.

Principle #5: Give Pleasure to Others

In the last chapter, you were exposed to the idea that you're not just designed for receiving pleasure, but you also have the ability to give it to others. The slogan "One day at a time" together with the principle of giving pleasure to others is like adding chocolate syrup to ice cream: The syrup takes an already good idea and makes it even better.

On a separate piece of paper or in a journal, I want you to take a moment and write down some ideas as to how you might be good at giving pleasure to others.

Let's take this just a little further. Who are the people you're most likely to give pleasure to on a daily basis in your life? Write out their names.

To really make pleasuring others a lifestyle, I recommend that you keep track of it for a while. So in your journal, Palm Pilot, or calendar, make a short note of what you're doing toward this goal.

As you continue to track this, you'll begin to see the pleasure lifestyle take over your daily routine. We all know that every journey is undertaken one step at a time, and every great journey progresses one day at a time. I wish you the absolute best as you travel the path of pleasure.

❦ ❦ ❦

Chapter Thirteen

Your Pleasure Calendar

In the last chapter, you learned how to give yourself and others pleasure each day. That daily foundation prepares you as you get ready to construct a whole life of pleasure. At this time you're ready to start placing the beams and a roof on your new lifestyle. This is going to be a very fun house to build!

To make this project possible, you need to start with the primary pleasures you identified earlier in the book. For each zone of pleasure, I want you to list your top three specific pleasures on a separate piece of paper or in a journal.

Now this list is quite different from your daily pleasures in that these are the ones that don't have a time limit. If your soul likes to travel and see new sights, that could be on your list. If your body has the urge to whitewater raft, ski, climb, or just be still, write those activities down. Your spirit might want to study or visit a spiritual location, teach, or be involved in a quality and prolonged service of some type. All the pleasures that are primary to you will make up your list.

You see, these primary pleasures are uniquely yours. You've been designed in this way or have been exposed to them or their traditions, and they've been etched upon your life. Regardless of why it's so, these particular pleasures are now yours. They're the primary ones on your palette of pleasure.

It's with this unique palette that you'll create an amazing house of pleasure for yourself. The primary pleasures of your body, spirit, and soul constitute the beams and the roof. The secondary pleasures create the walls, colors, and aromas of your new home.

For now, we're going to focus on the core structure— the beams and the roof. When you regularly participate in or experience these pleasures, they fortify you and in many ways make you really feel that life is worth living.

Now that you've identified three of your top pleasures for each major pleasure zone, you have the beams and supporting material to create a frame, which is a very necessary thing to have when you're building something. To build and maintain a structure, you're going to have to make a decision: Is the power of pleasure something that you want in your life regardless of how you feel?

Imagine having to talk about wanting pleasure in your life! However, this is something that many people really have to think through. I compare this decision to the one involved in purchasing a new home. If you've been through the process of house shopping, you know what I mean.

You drive all over town looking at homes in your price range, as well as ones that aren't affordable that the Realtor thinks you'll really like. Then you pull up to "the" house—you know, the one that takes your breath away. *This is it!* You can feel it in your gut. The rooms are perfect, and the neighborhood and yard are just right. You go outside and the view is amazing.

Then after all this emotion comes that moment of decision. For some people, it's instantaneous; others come back to the house again and again, courting it as they would someone they were interested in romantically. Then the contract papers come, and you have to decide.

The Realtor wants you to sign here and initial there, there, and there—and don't forget the earnest money check. Now you're committed!

The same scenario is true of pleasure. You imagined this great "house" of pleasure. You've been courting the idea of having the power of pleasure as a part of your lifestyle. In your mind, you walked through the various rooms and saw some of the sights surrounding this house, but you have to commit.

The contract precedes the construction. After you sign on the dotted line, a house of pleasure can be built that's uniquely designed for you and decorated with your palette of pleasure.

On a separate piece of paper or in a journal, write: "I am committed to regularly engaging in my primary pleasures. I am committed to following through by scheduling these pleasures into my life." Add your signature and the date underneath.

All right, then with the paperwork out of the way, let's get to work. You want to have specific primary pleasures scheduled consistently. You'll have to decide what frequency is possible with regard to a particular pleasure while still maintaining the other two aspects of the triangle of balance (relationships and responsibilities).

So let's break these pleasure options down into time categories for you. You may have only one or several in each space, depending on your time availability, resources, stage of life, or specific pleasuring needs. On a separate piece of paper or in a journal, list the specific pleasures you'd like to have in your new life under each of the following categories:

- My Weekly Pleasure Options
- My Bimonthly Pleasure Options
- My Monthly Pleasure Options
- My Quarterly Pleasure Options
- My Biannual Pleasure Options
- My Annual Pleasure Options
- My Pleasure Options over the Next Few Years

I know that this schedule can be a challenge at first as you adopt a new lifestyle, but before long your appointments with pleasure will have the same value as the other ones you have to keep—such as those associated with your health, finances, and relationships.

You've accomplished quite a bit so far. Now let's get down to the very nitty-gritty. You'll need a calendar, Palm Pilot, or day planner. If you don't have one already, pick one up today so that you can proceed. Physically take your writing utensil in hand and boldly place the pleasures mentioned into the spaces available in your calendar. I know this is the real cruncher for some people. I see the 5 A.M. gym crowd doing their various pleasures because they, like me, have learned to prioritize pleasure and schedule it in. I've found that actually writing it in your day planner, Palm Pilot, or calendar is the difference between success and failure.

Just as the people building a house would have to schedule when they'll be on-site to actually do the job or oversee it, so it is with building your house of pleasure. You have to schedule it if you expect to get it accomplished. On a separate piece of paper or in a journal, write the date you scheduled your weekly, biweekly, monthly, quarterly, biannual, and annual pleasures.

You're really making progress in changing your life to include more pleasure. I want to encourage you a bit before we conclude our conversations on the power of pleasure. I want to assure you that once you build your house, you'll feel much safer. I know that many people create unnecessary stress due to poor planning.

Imagine a woman who doesn't have a lot of food but invites all the relatives over. She's stricken with anxiety over her situation. So it is with people who don't plan for pleasure. Their tanks are on empty. Then their life throws a curveball, and *whammo*—they have anxiety, because they don't know how they're going to make it.

These feelings aren't major issues for balanced pleasurers. You probably know at least one of these individuals. They're the folks who put the beams of scheduled pleasure in place by giving themselves and others pleasure daily. Life also throws them curveballs (actually, I think we all get them), but they have a totally different experience. Their tanks are full—they're having a good time, being responsible, and enjoying strong relationships.

They can take a curveball in stride. It might be painful, but they can absorb its impact more readily. If the curveball demands support from relationships, it's only a call away. If they need resources, they have them or can get them because their credit rating is acceptable.

So when you build the house of pleasure, there's much more comfort and safety in your life. As the curveballs come, you can rely on a foundation of pleasure that you already planned earlier and have something to look forward to.

I remember the year Lisa and I got thrown one of the biggest curveballs of our marriage, involving business and friendships. We were really hurting, but it just so happened that months before, we'd decided to go home to Pennsylvania to visit family over Thanksgiving. Due to our preplanning pleasure, we both were supported by loved ones and were able to utilize the power of pleasure to soften the blow.

When I look over our 20-year marriage, I can see several times when preplanning for pleasure really helped us get over several smaller bumps in the road. It seems that after we participated in these preplanned pleasures, our perception was more relaxed and the mountains turned back into the molehills that they really were.

The last idea I'd like to share with you after you've built your house of pleasure is vitally important. One of the smallest but most important pieces of equipment in your home is found on the door of every entrance. That's right—it's the lock. I know that the doorknob is important as well, but the lock is critical to protect your home, valuables, and loved ones from anyone with the intent to harm or steal from you.

As it is with your physical home, so it is with your house of pleasure: It's beautiful and strong, but if left unprotected, it could become damaged and even be destroyed. Now I wish that protecting your house were as easy as carrying around a lock. It's sad to say, but guarding it will take some work. First, it will require your learning a really important word—*no*. Yes, you need to say no to some of the crazy circumstances or people in your life.

Lisa and I live what I write about. We really try to form a plan and stick with it. We also make sure that our children get pleasure as regularly as they do food.

One Friday around 4 P.M. a parent stopped by with a last-minute invitation for one of our children to attend a birthday party the next day. We already had an activity planned for our whole family, which is one of the best pleasures of all for the Weisses. Now this very poorly organized, less-than-thoughtful parent may have had the expectation that we'd drop whatever we had scheduled because of her chaotic lifestyle and lack of planning.

176

Don't get me wrong: Lisa and I like this child and the family, but we had to make a decision. We decided if it were another day and we were given a decent amount of time, we would have loved to allow our child to purchase a gift and go to a party. However, as things stood, our decision was sadly a no.

Lisa and I had to protect the pleasure of *our* family from the chaos of that particular family. Now you will have legitimate reasons to change your plans from time to time. What I'm talking about is prioritizing your scheduled pleasures. If you start making your or other people's crises a reason to forfeit an enjoyable activity, you'll find that pleasure starts becoming eroded from your life.

Protecting your pleasure can come in the form of a good friend whom you call to help you distinguish between the valid and less-than-valid reasons to cancel a pleasure appointment. I know that some of my clients set up a small consequence if they call one off.

Regardless of how you safeguard your pleasure, I'd encourage you to think about this: Every house is incomplete without a lock, and every life of pleasure is incomplete without protection.

❦

I hope that you really enjoyed our travels together. I can only imagine your face as you thought through the different processes: *Am I an overpleasurer, an underpleasurer, or a balanced pleasurer? Is my triangle well-balanced?* Hopefully you smiled as you walked down memory lane, discovering your past pleasures and your pleasure hierarchy. You learned how to pleasure daily, pleasure others, and pleasure always.

You're an amazing person who was created for infinite pleasure. You can unleash its power in order to have more fun, conquer difficult issues, and fortify yourself against the storms of life. Your pleasure palette is uniquely yours—there's nobody with exactly the same one. You can create incredible colors of pleasure that only you can enjoy fully.

I encourage you to deeply experience the power of pleasure . . . let your very cells feel the invigoration of a life of pleasure. Those around you will be changed as your pleasuring through word or deed blows around them like a cool, Colorado morning breeze.

You're on the adventure of a lifetime—*your* lifetime! Your journey starts now, and I wish you the best.

ॐ ॐ ॐ

Afterword

I hope that you enjoyed the ride on the river of pleasure and have had some excitement blow into your life now that you understand how you're created for pleasure.

I know that at times you had to dig in your heels as you worked through various ideas and systems. That's what I call paddling on the river of pleasure. You're worth every minute of self-discovery you invested in this trip.

You can now see your life with more hope and know that you're able to draw on the power of pleasure. You have the experience of identifying your unique pleasure hierarchy. You're also aware of how to utilize the power of pleasure to create a more fun and fulfilled you! I know that this will not only impact you, but also everyone in the boat of life along with you.

Yes, your family, friends, co-workers, and neighbors will see you as a happier person. In addition, you'll find that people are more attracted to you because you're actually more fun to be with! So as an experienced rafter on the pleasure river, I encourage you to schedule your pleasure experiences regularly. You're worthy of the maximum pleasure in life.

You're now the navigator of your own boat. You understand how to capitalize on the power of pleasure and let the current continue to move you on down the river.

As you travel, you'll probably encounter people who want to join you on your journey, so bask in the company of fellow travelers . . . and, as always, enjoy the ride. It's been my pleasure to be your guide. If I can be of any further help, feel free to contact my office. I wish you happy trails during your lifelong journey experiencing the power of pleasure.

— **Douglas Weiss, Ph.D.**

About the Author

Douglas Weiss, Ph.D., is an international lecturer, is the author of 20 books, and has been in clinical practice for more than 18 years. He is the executive director of Heart to Heart Counseling Center in Colorado Springs, Colorado.

At the Center, Dr. Weiss and a team of private practitioners offer 3-Day Intensives for couples and individuals, as well as telephone counseling. Dr. Weiss has appeared regularly in the print and broadcast media and has been featured as a clinical expert on *Oprah, Good Morning America, 20/20,* and many other national shows.

Dr. Weiss lives in Colorado Springs with his wife, Lisa; their two children, Hadassah and Jubal; and a spunky Afghan hound, Moses. To contact Dr. Weiss, call Heart to Heart Counseling Center at 719-278-3708 or e-mail: **heart 2heart@xc.org**. Website: **www.thepowerofpleasure.net**

❦ ❦ ❦

We hope you enjoyed this Hay House book.
If you'd like to receive a free catalog featuring
additional Hay House books and products, or
if you'd like information about the
Hay Foundation, please contact:

Hay House, Inc.
P.O. Box 5100
Carlsbad, CA 92018-5100

(760) 431-7695 or (800) 654-5126
(760) 431-6948 (fax) or (800) 650-5115 (fax)
www.hayhouse.com® • www.hayfoundation.org

Published and distributed in Australia by: Hay House Australia Pty.
Ltd., 18/36 Ralph St., Alexandria NSW 2015 • *Phone:* 612-9669-4299
Fax: 612-9669-4144 • www.hayhouse.com.au

Published and distributed in the United Kingdom by: Hay House
UK, Ltd., 292B Kensal Rd., London W10 5BE • *Phone:*
44-20-8962-1230 • *Fax:* 44-20-8962-1239 • www.hayhouse.co.uk

Published and distributed in the Republic of South Africa by:
Hay House SA (Pty), Ltd., P.O. Box 990, Witkoppen 2068
Phone/Fax: 27-11-706-6612 • orders@psdprom.co.za

Published in India by: Hay House Publishers India,
Muskaan Complex, Plot No. 3, B-2, Vasant Kunj, New Delhi 110 070
Phone: 91-11-4176-1620 • *Fax:* 91-11-4176-1630
www.hayhouseindia.co.in

Distributed in Canada by: Raincoast, 9050 Shaughnessy St.,
Vancouver, B.C. V6P 6E5 • *Phone:* (604) 323-7100
Fax: (604) 323-2600 • www.raincoast.com

Tune in to **HayHouseRadio.com®** for the best in inspirational
talk radio featuring top Hay House authors! And, sign up
via the Hay House USA Website to receive the Hay House
online newsletter and stay informed about what's going
on with your favorite authors. You'll receive bimonthly
announcements about Discounts and Offers, Special Events,
Product Highlights, Free Excerpts, Giveaways, and more!
www.hayhouse.com®